What Really Happened in Northern Ireland's Counterinsurgency: Revision and Revelation

Political, social, and economic programs are usually more valuable than conventional military operations in addressing the root causes of conflict and undermining an insurgency.
— *The U.S. Army/Marine Corps Counterinsurgency Field Manual*[1]

The cultural characteristics of the British Army set it up for success in counterinsurgency operations.
— *Lieutenant Colonel Robert M. Cassidy, U.S. Army*[2]

The British Army has excelled in small-unit anti-guerrilla warfare as they did in other aspects of counterinsurgency.
— *Thomas R. Mockaitis*[3]

The idea that the British are masters of counterinsurgency is very dated.
— *Major General Paul Newton, joint head of Force Strategic Engagement Cell in Iraq*[4]

The Search for Victorious Models

The stubborn insurgencies in Afghanistan and Iraq have sparked searches for successful counterinsurgent lessons from around the world. In addition to studying America's experience in the Vietnam War, most often U.S. students of foreign counterinsurgencies look to European powers—particularly Britain, France, and to a much less degree, Portugal— all of which fought several national liberation fronts or people's wars against non-Western nationalists, guerrillas, or communists across the globe to retain their colonies.[5] Often this investigation has centered on universal "lessons" of counterinsurgency that can be applied anywhere. Other taxonomies have sought out particular techniques to be applied selectively to combating irregular warfare, such as resettling the local population out of reach of the guerrillas, securing porous borders, gathering intelligence, and meeting peoples' basic needs.[6]

By the same token, American students of counterinsurgency (COIN) have generally neglected non-Western cases such as Algeria's suppression of Islamist forces during the 1990s, Syria's crushing of combatants during Lebanon's civil war, or Israel's experiences against terrorism and insurgency.[7]

Instead, American practitioners, scholars, and civilian analysts have most often studied British counterinsurgency methods because, in part, Britain has fought a number of insurgencies in the 20th century and also because British officers and officials (as well as pro-British foreigners) have promoted their expertise in waging anti-insurgent campaigns. From its rich history, the "British have a better track record in counterinsurgency than any other nation."[8] Before its 20th century low-intensity conflicts against insurgents or terrorists, Britain fought many small-scale campaigns in colonial wars in the Middle East, Africa, Afghanistan, India, and of course in North America against its rebellious colonies. Additionally, it turned the tables against the French in the Peninsular War in Spain with a smallish land force working with Spanish guerrillas in its own version of irregular warfare against Napoleon's occupying army.

These conflicts together with geopolitical realities contributed to Britain's predisposition for small wars and imperial expeditions as London policed its far-flung empire. Consequently, British history is replete with military experiences in suppressing colonial resistance, fighting guerrillas, and man-hunting bandits. Some admirers of the British way of war have gone so far as to advance the notion that culture and organization "made the British Army amenable to changes required to successfully counter insurgencies or control internal unrest."[9] This tradition of successful low-intensity warfare, so it was argued, even transcended the impact of Britain's large-scale conventional conflicts in World War I and II, the Korean War, and the Falkland campaign. Even as late as the mid-1990s, another expert writing in *Parameters* concluded: "The experience of numerous small wars has provided the British Army with a unique insight into this demanding form [counterinsurgency] of conflict."[10]

Several macro-level factors shaped Britain's military structure. Being an island nation, Britain looked to naval forces as its main line of defense, lavishing funding on the Royal Navy and consequently scrimping on a large standing army. This pattern differed from Britain's continental rivals, such as Austria, France, and Prussia (the latter of which formed the nucleus of a powerful German nation by the 19th century's end). Revolutionary France's reliance on large massed forces, as distinct from the small 18th century professional armies, accentuated Britain's variance with its adversaries across the English Channel. As the continental powers entered into the industrial age, their mass manufacturing capacity enabled them to field powerful armies with heavy artillery and then tanks and trucks—all reliant on railroad transport. With a different set of geopolitical circumstances, Britain hewed to its traditional approach of large fleets, small ground forces, and civilian colonial services to police its far-flung imperial holdings.

During the formative 19th-century small-war environment, Britain relied almost exclusively on a slender professional officer corps drawn mostly from the lower aristocracy and from volunteers in its enlisted ranks for its pocket-sized land force, while its Continental rivals resorted to conscription to amass big land armies. The British stuck with volunteers in the regimental system, which one admirer characterized as "a quasi-tribal" because of its long-term cohesiveness and *esprit de corps* that isolated the officers and other ranks from the "slings and arrows" of the largely unsympathetic civilian population.[11] But these aficionados of British military institutions missed the baronial origins of the regimental system, its subsidy by super-wealthy earls and lords, and its dilettante officers who purchased their commissions, resulting in such disasters as the destructive charge of the Light Brigade "into the mouth of Hell" during the Crimean War.[12] Not until after near-decimation of the "noble six hundred" did Britain undertake serious reform and professionalization of its regiments.

Yet the idiosyncratic regimental tradition did not die away in the aftermath of the brief mid-19th century conflict in the Russian Crimea. As late as World War II, the noted British novelist Evelyn Waugh wrote tongue-in-cheek about transforming recruits into regimental tribes: "The discipline of the square, the tradition of the mess, would work their magic and *esprit de corps* would fall like blessed unction from above."[13] These drum beats fashioned "tribesmen" from individuals coming from all walks of life, rather than larger conventional U.S. Army divisions of the world wars.

Once World War I ended, Britain returned to its pre-war model of small forces strewn around the global, relying on Indian manpower to hold the subcontinent, to first oust the Turks from Iraq, and then to put down an Iraqi insurrection during the late 1920s. Empire on the cheap sometimes backfired, however. By relying, for example, on the sweepings of society to defeat rebellions they wound up with thugs to fill the ranks, as when the infamous Black and Tan units were used to suppress post-World War I Irish nationalists rather than deploying a large regular army, as we shall see. Elsewhere the spirit of unconventional warfare remained alive.

Taking a leaf from Lawrence of Arabia's experiences in World War I, the eccentric British officer Orde Wingate imparted guerrilla warfare techniques, not to Arab tribesmen as had T. E. Lawrence but to Jewish residents in the Holy Land during the interwar period. He passed along ambush and raid tactics in the 1930s to Jewish special night squads against the Arabs in Palestine before attaining fame in World War II.[14] Later when war broke out with Germany and Japan, Wingate was well versed in commando operations which he applied in an Asian theater. In Burma, Wingate organized and led the fabled Chindits in deep-penetration raids against Japanese communication lines.[15]

During World War II, many British troops gained experience in small-unit unconventional warfare with the formation of special units, such as Special Air Service (SAS), Special Boat Section (SBS), and the Long Range Desert Group (LRDG) together with those (resistance operators) commanded by the Special Operations Executive (SOE).[16] Combining ships, landing craft, seaborne infantry, and paratroopers before and after its retreat from Dunkirk, Britain launched a series of audacious commando raids in Norway, France, Italy, and the Levant prior to the Anglo-American D-Day operation on the Normandy coast.[17] Even small missions amid the total symmetrical warfare in the course of 1939–1945 were dealt with by compact specialized units tasked for unconventional operations. These units and experience lent themselves to the exigencies of insurgent conflicts after the war.

Another element in Britain's adaptability to insurrectionists stemmed from the paradoxical condition that its counterinsurgency army possessed limited resources. In fact, British overseas forces had almost always been strapped for troops, equipment, and firepower. The empire, in fact, had been ruled cheaply for centuries. In waging wars against saboteurs and gunmen, who operate among the civilian population, more often than not employing fewer resources is better than using too much power. It compelled the military and the police to fight "smarter" rather than rely on massive doses of firepower, which often kill collaterally innocent bystanders. British officers are quick to note that the political, psychological, and propaganda dimensions count for more than the kinetic element of these largely politico-armed conflicts.

The post-World War II operational environment witnessed a profusion of low-intensity conflicts as weaker forces, be they anticolonial nationalists, Communist insurgents, or terrorist bands, took on their much more powerful adversaries around the world. Many countries underwent these less-than-conventional wars. But Britain weathered several of these asymmetrical campaigns in its colonies. Thus, British counterinsurgency practices have received glowing adulation, especially from American students particularly of their methods in Malaya.[18]

The Malaya campaign's favorable outcome impacted American thinking about peoples' war first in Vietnam and then beyond. British authors, such as Robert Thompson, the Permanent Secretary of Defense for Malaya, in his influential book, *Defeating Communist Insurgency*, laid out the winning strategy in Malaya.[19] From January 1952 to May 1954 the man-on-the-spot was General Gerard Templer, an infantry and armor officer who was a veteran of both world wars. General Templer devised or implemented the political policies that led to victory. He famously stated that "the answer [to the insurgency]

> [General Templer] famously stated that "the answer [to the insurgency] lies not in pouring more troops into the jungle, but in the hearts and minds of the people."

lies not in pouring more troops into the jungle, but in the hearts and minds of the people."[20]

Possibly no single catch-phrase epitomized the orientation of the military forces toward their adversaries and, more importantly, the population "sea" in which the guerrilla "fish" must "swim," as Mao Tse-tung so memorably put it. In short, the population must be won over to the government side against the insurgents or the military effort will fail. Western armies cannot easily adopt the ancient Roman response to rebellion by scorching the earth and putting entire towns to the sword as Tacitus noted in *Agricola*. This famous Roman historian recorded a Caledonian (the Latin name for Scottish) rebel inciting his followers by cataloging Rome's devastating barbarity and unforgettably uttering: "They [the Romans] make a desert and call it peace."[21] The mass-murder of insurgents and their population "sea" (whether by Rome or other states) violates American principles. Having ruled out extermination, U.S. military forces have turned to ways to win over populations while they pursue insurgents.

Thus American practitioners looked for model and direction to Britain, which fought scores of small wars in pursuit of empire and boasted most often of its exemplars in Malaya and Northern Ireland. In Malaya, General Templer set about initiating many of the tactics that have since served as a model for counterinsurgency. The so-called Malayan Emergency, for example, witnessed the resettlement of ethnic Chinese away from jungles and outside the reach of the Chinese-dominated guerrilla forces. It also saw the direct appeal to all non-Malays, who represented a pool of recruits for the Communist insurgents, by granting them citizenship to dry up their grievances against their adopted homeland. British troops and their Malay auxiliaries were generally restrained in the use of their firepower so as not to recruit for the guerrillas by killing innocents. Templer's efforts have long been enshrined in the heraldry of COIN medallions. But on a less lofty level, these stratagems were classic divide-and-rule approaches that Britain and other colonial officers learned in public school from the readings of ancient practitioners of war such as Julius Caesar.[22] They used them to great effect in the Third World as Caesar did against the quarrelsome Gauls two millennia earlier.

As it turned out, Anglophiles read much into the history and qualities of British fighting forces. Some waxed rhapsodic about Britain's unique cultural characteristics for combating insurgent-like violence. One enthusiastic exponent of Britain's guerrilla fighting went so far as to contend: "British success in counterinsurgency is also attributable to British society, which had created an Army 'ideally suited to counterinsurgency and to cultural attitudes about how that Army might be used'."[23] Given Britain's extensive operational experience in dealing with insurgencies after World War II in such places as Palestine, Cyprus, Kenya, Oman, Borneo, and Malaya, it is puzzling to confront the fact of how long it took to implement the proper tactics in Northern Ireland of the late 1960s and early 1970s, as will be sketched below.

These trumpeters of British counterinsurgency prowess often implied criticism of American efforts. They lauded the British army for "employing minimum forces … by inserting small patrols that operate like the insurgents, not with airpower and artillery."[24] This same author went on to contend that: "The British Army does not try to avoid casualties, and it does not seem to be averse to taking them."[25] In surveying British campaigns from Malaya to Dhofar, this analyst writing in another work held that: "The most salient common characteristic of these campaigns was how successful the British Army was in conducting small-scale and medium-scale operations" and by implicit extension how poorly post-World War II American forces have fought irregular wars.[26]

The lavishly praised techniques of the British Army in Northern Ireland were deemed applicable to the blast-furnace streets of Iraq. The acclaimed British military historian John Keegan opined: "As the entry into Basra was to prove, the British army's mastery of the methods of urban warfare is transferable. What had worked in Belfast could be made to work also in Basra, against another set of urban terrorists, with a different motivation from the Irish Republicans though equally nasty."[27] Until recently this represents the prevailing consensus about Britain's counterinsurgency prowess in Northern Ireland and elsewhere.

Nonetheless, it is argued here that U.S. counterinsurgency successes in Iraq dating from at least the 2007 "surge," which employed not only 28,500 additional combat troops but also sound anti-insurgent tactics and nationwide political astuteness, has earned American forces belated recognition for their nonkinetic approaches to winning over Sunni tribesmen and calming Iraq's sectarian bloodshed. This achievement alone disproves much implied criticism—both cultural and organizational—contained in references praising Britain's antiguerrilla practices as being innately and almost exclusively a British province. Yet, the British Army's serious missteps in Northern Ireland had to be overcome, not with organizational culture indoctrination but with "a comprehensive training package provided by the Northern Ireland Training Team to each and every British infantry battalion that deployed to the province from 1972 onwards."[28]

Also in Iraq, Britain's reputation for waging counterinsurgency operations suffered a body blow in its lengthening Basra campaign, as its troops remained aloof while gangs and militias preyed on the citizens of Iraq's second largest city.[29] Nor have British efforts in Afghanistan recaptured the Malaya luster.[30]

Rather than dealing with Iraq or Afghanistan, this essay seeks to strip away some of the overly varnished veneer from the Northern Ireland example or at a minimum present a deeper understanding of Britain's much proclaimed counterinsurgency effectiveness in attaining peace and stability. Let us look beneath the plaudits for the British Army's small-unit patrolling and keen intelligence capability to examine what changes took place within the society itself to bring about tranquility and peace to that troubled corner of Ireland.

A Bit of History

Britain's experience in Northern Ireland demands some historical context to make sense of London's programs and responses in what became known as the "Troubles" at the start of the late 1960s. Like many bitter internal conflicts, the Irish-British antagonism is imbued with a deep and convoluted history. If much of the complex detail has little relevance to the Special Operations Forces community, something needs to be written about the general picture prior to the Troubles.

The Anglo-Irish antagonism is rooted in a colonial experience embedded with religious discrimination flowing from an extended chapter in Ireland's history. Even a brief account requires reaching back into Ireland's misty past and its relations with the larger island to its east. England's first large-scale invasion of the land across the Irish Sea dates all the way back to the year 1172, when Henry II led a formidable invading force to consolidate his hold over earlier waves of Norman adventurers as well as the native Irish population. As such, Henry's intervention constituted a continuation of the Norman Conquest of England that originated a hundred years before with the battle of Hastings in 1066. More importantly, Henry's invasion touched off a series of conquistadorial enterprises that left the Emerald Isle bloody, vengeful, and hate-filled for all things English in the centuries to come. Some of these ancient hatreds were mitigated by centuries of intermingling of the native Irish and the English interlopers. Succeeding influxes of English and Scots settlers were assimilated into the broader Irish culture through intermarriage and acculturation. But the historical record itself, despite the physical incorporation, served the ends of future rebels, who legitimately pointed at London's bloodstained legacy in Ireland.

> *... the historical record ... served the ends of future rebels, who legitimately pointed at London's bloodstained legacy in Ireland.*

When the English monarchy under Henry VIII broke with the Pope and Roman Catholicism and established a state Protestant church in England in the 1530s, the religious difference between Anglo overlords and Irish subjects soon threw fresh salt into colonial wounds of the Irish populations who witnessed conquest, subjugation, and displacement from their lands. Now the conquerors' religion differed from the conquered, and sectarianism added another ruinous dimension to the relationship. Henry and his successor Tudor monarchs (Edward VI, Mary, and Elizabeth) completed the subjugation of Ireland and ensured for nearly 400 years that its government would be English. They feared that Ireland, with its anti-English sentiments and anti-Protestant beliefs, would open its territory to European enemies of the English crown. As history shows, this was a genuine danger.

The Catholic-Protestant cleavages, however, mattered most in Northern Ireland due to a twist of fate. Political disturbances in and around the northern province of Ulster plagued Elizabeth I in the late 16th century. Recalcitrant local lords, aided by Catholic Spain and Spanish troops, resisted English rule, which ultimately prevailed but only after London's colonial settlements took root. Huge swaths of land were confiscated by the English queen, which her successor James I resolved to resettle with a significant number of English farmers and Lowland Scots to achieve stability and safety from foreign interventions. The cultural and religious differences in Northern Ireland date from this settlement or "planting" of non-Irish peoples in what was termed the Ulster Plantation.[31]

The use of settlers to stabilize unruly regions is a time-polished practice seen in lands around the world. As in the case of Northern Ireland, settling foreigners on seized territory often sows dragons' teeth that in time germinate tragedies, exemplified in ethnic cleansing, intersectarian violence, and territorial blood feuds spanning the globe. Northern Ireland was a prime example of this effect. At inception, the English crown's grant of territory was extremely attractive to Protestant immigrants, who recognized that land constituted the source of wealth and the basis of power and prestige. To facilitate this "planting" scheme, the London government confiscated much of the land in six northern counties—Armagh, Cavan, Coleraine (later renamed Londonderry or Derry), Donegal, Fermanagh, and Tyrone—laying the basis for sectarian strife and the "Troubles" three and a half centuries later. It then granted patches of land from one to two thousand acres at inexpensive rents, with the requirements that the recipient then settle Protestant tenants to cultivate the soil and build castles to defend the surrounding territory.

Thus began the "plantation" of Protestant settlers from the Scottish lowlands and the English countryside, who leveled forests, farmed, built churches, schools, and markets, thereby creating a new society that was alien to Irish ways. The displaced native Irish populations moved to the worst lands and became either tenants of the newcomers or their laborers, losing status and income. Naturally, they grew intensely resentful about their fate at the hand of the interlopers. Subsequent events, too many and too intricate to recount in this summary, entrenched the Protestant hold on wealth and power in the northern corner of Ireland that lasted to the present times.

Religion now infused itself into the tangled Irish landscape adding the feature of the Catholic-Protestant conflict to Ireland's history of opposition to English domination. When, for example, English notables invited William of Orange (a Protestant monarch from the Dutch principality of Orange) to invade England and oust Catholic ruler James II, the conflict spilled over to Ireland. After fleeing to France, James resolved to capture Ireland, (with aid of his local coreligious brethren) as a bridgehead for a victorious return to England. William thus crossed the Irish Sea and attacked the deposed king and his Irish Catholic and French troops. William's army—comprised of Protestant troops from Ulster, England, Denmark, and Holland—won a decisive battle at the Boyne River in 1690, a victory that is still celebrated today by the Orange Order in Ulster by staging provocative annual marches through Catholic neighborhoods in Belfast.

The wearing of the green or the orange in contemporary Ireland, therefore, carries religious and political significance stretching back 300 years to a battle fought a century before the United States declared its independence from Great Britain. The Protestant-dominated counties surrounding the Belfast harbor evolved into a pro-British enclave. There the Catholic minority and the Protestant majority in the northern enclave tensely coexisted, being segregated by religion and power as well as loyalties to the English crown or to the Roman papacy.

The remainder of Ireland also suffered under British rule with episodes of repression followed by callous neglect. A monstrous example of Britain's studied indifference occurred in the mid-19th century when famine befell

Ireland. By 1841, two thirds of the Irish people depended on agriculture for their livelihood. Most survived as tenant farmers on lands held by landlords, who cared little for their renters' welfare. These impoverished rural populations relied on the abundance of potatoes for their sustenance. Disaster struck in 1842, when a fungus partially destroyed the potato harvest. The conservative government of Robert Peel responded thoughtfully by subsidizing relief (i.e., welfare) projects to hire destitute farmers, allowing them to purchase food. Next the Peel government took the momentous step of repealing the corn (i.e., grain) laws in all of the United Kingdom, which for centuries prohibited the importation of grain and protected English farmers from cheaper grains produced abroad. This free-trade measure caused his government to lose power because the landed interests rebelled at Peel's free-trade policies. The incoming Whig administration of Lord John Russell rigidly applied the prevailing notions of *laissez faire,* which meant no government interference in the nation's economy. If the Irish peasantry died because the British treasury refused to buy food, so be it. The economy's imbalances would be sorted out in due course by market forces alone.

When the potato harvest wilted again due to another blight in 1846, the English government initially stood aside while the Irish starved, perished, and faced extinction. When the crown's officials finally acted in the face of prolonged famine, typhus, and epidemic fevers, it was with the callousness, parsimoniousness, and self-righteousness that Charles Dickens portrayed in his contemporaneous novels.[32] The disaster killed a million and a half people out of a population of eight million and drove another million to the New World, where they settled on the Eastern seaboard mainly in and around Boston. From these destitute immigrants sprang an anti-English colony within the United States that repeatedly twisted the British lion's tail, aided their fellow countrymen across the Atlantic, and even clandestinely funded their arms purchases in the mid-20th century to kill British soldiers in the streets of Belfast.[33]

A complete retelling of this story takes us too far from the intent of this essay. Suffice to write that anything as horrific as the great famine could not but gravely impact the course of Anglo-Irish relations.[34] London's willful dismissal of its colonial responsibilities, after centuries of misrule, did nothing but fan the flames of Irish resistance at a time when European nationalism erupted across the continent in the Austrian-ruled Italy and

Hungary, the fragmented German states, and the turbulent Balkans. The heady brew of nationalism—the desire for ethnic independence and separate identity—proved as intoxicating to the Irish as it did to the Tuscans, Lombards, Prussians, Serbians, and Croatians of the same historical period.

The Birth of Modern Irish Nationalism

A sense of Irishness and resentment of over-harsh British colonialism fused into fervent demands for independence from the crown's governance. Post-famine Ireland groped failingly at first and then powerfully toward a means for independence from Britain's tyranny. Poverty, backwardness, grievances, and the famine's memory fueled the island's majority with a passion for liberty. In the northeast corner in Ulster, however, the tight-knit Protestant community cherished its union with Britain. Unlike the rest of Ireland, Ulster underwent an industrial revolution similar to those occurring in Manchester, Leeds, Liverpool, and Glasgow. Like England and Scotland, ship building, manufacturing, and linen production took root in Belfast reinforcing the religious-political connection with Britain through economic ties. The lands beyond the Ulster province stagnated, giving rise to explosive independence sentiments. To Ulster's south, the Irish towns and countryside teemed with leagues, brotherhoods, secret military organizations, and other nationalist movements to press the case for reform of the tenant-landlord laws and ultimately independence from Britain.

This upwelling of nationalism found expression in demands for home rule. From the mid-19th century to the establishment of the Irish Free State in the 1920s, Ireland erupted in strife. The struggle for sovereignty pursued two separate paths: one road passed through constitutional and parliamentary steps; and the other flowed underground through revolution and conspiracy that would, in time, plunge Ireland into bloody conflict. Some British governments attempted to preempt burgeoning Irish demands to be masters of their own destiny by transferring local powers to an Irish parliament toward home rule (i.e., autonomy). But these late-19th-century concessions foundered on Protestant-dominated Ulster's insistence on maintaining its union with Britain and on British conservative politicians who viewed concessions as surrender of imperial interests and betrayal of the loyalists in Northern Ireland. Many twists and turns followed these early efforts to address what became known as the Irish Question.[35]

Ireland seethed with independence fever at the beginning of the 20th century. Literary societies infused Irish nationalism with Gaelic literature, histories, and poetry. From this fermenting milieu emerged Sinn Fein (meaning "We Our Selves")—a full-fledged separatist movement advocating a total break with any political connections to the British crown. Sinn Fein squared off against those Irish politicians seeking merely home rule and continued political bonds with Britain. Others joined the Irish Volunteers, a militia whose ranks opposed British governance and longed to de-Anglicize the whole of Ireland. As a disturbing sign of things to come, more private armies also formed in other parts of the country.

Up north, the Ulsterites fought any notion of home rule for Ireland, which envisioned the Northern Ireland enclave controlled by the rest of the Irish population to its south. These Orangemen stood up the Ulster Volunteers, a militia, and secured secreted arms from a Germany all too willing to cause its British adversary trouble in its own backyard. Despite the rising ferment in greater Ireland for its own sovereignty, the outbreak of World War I squelched consideration of home rule in London for the duration of the war. But in Ireland itself, Britain's absorption in the conflict against Germany and her allies presented a rare opportunity for the Irish to take action. These Republicans started preparations for revolution as fighting on the Western Front preoccupied London. Militias drilled in Dublin while Germany laid plans to supply them with rifles, just as Berlin had earlier shipped arms to the Republicans' enemies in the north.

The day after Easter Sunday in 1916 a poorly executed insurrection of some 1,500 Irish Volunteers and other private military bands took place when they marched to the General Post Office building in central Dublin. The rebels occupied, defended, and proclaimed an independent republic from the post office buildings. In a near-suicidal clash, the rebels held off a much larger loyalist force of volunteers and regular British Army troops for 6 days before surrendering. Their rebellion backfired among many ordinary Irish citizens who considered the insurrectionists little more than backstabbers and even traitors because they had relatives and friends fighting alongside British regiments in France.

Then in a negative "lesson" to all counterinsurgency forces, the British snatched defeat from the jaws of victory by meting out firing-squad deaths to 15 rebel prisoners, including one wounded and chair-bound leader. British soldiers also angrily assaulted passers-by in the streets, shot a well-known pacifist, arrested 2,000 Republicans and Sinn Feiners, and imprisoned many without trials, who were innocent of the insurrection. These acts of revenge rather than deliberative justice washed back on the perpetrators. Opinions shifted among Ireland's population, who soon came to see those they had considered hooligans and rabble-rousers now as martyred heroes to Irish grievances against tyrannical British rule.

In London, cooler heads soon prevailed, and the British government backtracked on the excesses in the wake of the Easter Rebellion. Britain needed Irish recruits for the war against Germany and Austria-Hungary and for favorable American opinion so as to gain the United States entry into the war on the Allied side. To placate the resentful Irish nationalist sentiments, the British released the rebel internees. Among them was Eamon de Valera, the only Easter Rising commandant to escape the firing squad. Soon afterwards, De Valera as the leader of the Sinn Fein turned his aim against the moderate Home Rulers, ending over time any possible maintenance of ties between Ireland and Britain. Ireland now moved inexorably toward complete independence from Britain, with the Sinn Fein spearheading the drive. First, Sinn Fein members won local elections and then asserted their cause of Irish freedom.

Tensions between Irish political figures bent on breaking with Britain and the crown's officials and police finally descended into a shooting war of liberation in January 1919. The former Irish Volunteers, who participated in the Easter Rebellion, renamed themselves the Irish Republic Army (IRA) and initiated an insurgency by shooting soldiers and policemen, ambushing military trucks, assassinating suspected spies and informers, and raiding government armories in what became known as the Anglo-Irish War. The fighting seeped into Ulster, where Protestants, also known as Unionists, fought alongside British Army troops to maintain the "union" with the rest of the British Isles.

Rather than responding with classic counterinsurgency practices to win over Irish hearts and minds, as so many British officers would later advocate in our time, the Army responded ruthlessly to IRA provocations.

British authorities decided to meet terrorism with terrorism. They recruited unemployed former servicemen and sent them across the Irish Sea to reinforce the beleaguered police force. Uniformed in dark green caps and khaki trousers, these counter-guerrilla squads acquired the nickname of the Black and Tans and, more importantly, a legendary reputation for savage conduct. The Black and Tans tortured and sometimes executed prisoners. These harsh tactics soon turned the population totally against the British government. Likewise in the Ulster province, assassination was met with assassination in a "dirty war" of revenge and counter-revenge.

The Anglo-Irish War deserves more attention in U.S. military circles, for it foreshadowed many of the techniques later employed in peoples' war and insurgencies around the globe. Ireland was the first modern victim of British imperialism and colonialism to fight an effective guerrilla war of liberation (the American colonies were *the* first). The IRA cleverly turned Britain's post-World War I policies that favored the dismemberment of the Austro-Hungarian and Turkish empires against London. It exploited the widespread anti-imperialistic impulses during the early interwar years in many Western quarters. Within the British Isles themselves, public opinion, encouraged by the press, university professors, and some clergymen, swung toward acceptance of Irish nationalism. Officials, however, sought to justify retention of Ireland, as a domino whose fall would lead to dissolution of the entire British Empire.

Faced with an intractable insurgency and dissolving domestic support, British politicians groped for an acceptable settlement for both the Protestant enclave in Northern Ireland and the greater Catholic majority amid the gun battles, deadly raids, and street murders. Finally, London negotiated directly with Sinn Fein for a truce in July 1921. Make no bones about it—"the British Government had already been forced to accept political and moral defeat" even if perhaps the Republicans "were beginning to smell military defeat." [36]

The Anglo-Irish treaty ended up dividing 6 counties of Ulster from the remaining 26 counties to the south. This satisfied the Ulsterites but not the Irish Republicans, who wanted a united Gaelic Ireland entirely free from British rule, language, and custom in the North as well as the South. In the end the Republicans settled on just the Irish Free State, a Dominion within the British Commonwealth, without the Northern Ireland corner. London turned over the instruments of power in the South and withdrew from its oldest colony, which it had held for nearly 800 years.[37] Later the Irish Free State went the full shot by breaking all British ties and becoming the Republic of Ireland. The Irish Question assumed another form, however.

Despite the historic turn of events, the Anglo-Irish treaty constituted little more than a hostile and uneasy truce, for it left unresolved the unity of a partitioned Ireland, the continuation of British rule in Ulster, and the Protestant dominion over the Catholic minority in the Six Counties. It also left the cult of the gunmen as the historical legacy from the 1916–1922 war in both Ulster and the Irish Free State. It profoundly shaped the political and economic conditions in Ulster where it bred the conditions for an insurgency 40 years later.

The Northern Ireland Problem

Throughout the 1950s into the early 1960s, Northern Ireland remained a fundamentally divided and sectarian society.

— *Thomas Hennessey*[38]

Northern Ireland constituted an odd political configuration for its one and a half million inhabitants. At the time of partition from the Irish Free State in 1920, Ulster's Catholic minority comprised 33 percent of the population, but within the Six Counties themselves specific localities and towns sometimes held lopsided Catholic majorities. Some among the Catholic population longed for geographical and nationalistic unity with greater Ireland and detested inclusion within the United Kingdom of England, Scotland, and Wales. Conversely, the Protestant majority determined through employment practices and political discrimination to drive out the minority, or at the least subdue Catholic, or Nationalist, political aspirations. Through Unionist imposition of gerrymandering of election districts and plural votes for business property, the Catholic minority lost political power in electing Ministers of Parliament (MPs or representatives) to Britain's Parliament in Westminster and to the Ulster parliament at Stormont as well as local councils, which allocated jobs, housing, and social welfare. Successive Stormont governments gave short shrift to Catholic districts where chronic unemployment of near 40 percent persisted for decades, engendering frustration and enmity.

Unlike disputes in the Balkans or within Israel, land and boundaries were less an issue among the religious blocs. But like the black-white friction in the United States, tension within Ulster arose over genuine democracy and fair access to housing, jobs, and education. In short, the duel revolved around equality within the state. Sectarian distinctions overrode social and economic issues, undermining the genuine practice of democracy, similar to that witnessed in contemporary Iraq between voting blocs of Shia, Sunni, and Kurds. Voters cast ballots for Unionist (Protestant) or Nationalist (Catholic) candidates on the basis of religious affiliation rather than for politicians or parties appealing to broad-based constituencies. The majority ensured that Northern Ireland, in effect, functioned as a one-party state with the Unionist Party in the driver's seat from 1920 until recent years.

Adding to the sense of political grievance by the minority population was the makeup and behavior of the security forces. The Ulster Special Constabulary recruited the vast majority of its constables from Protestant neighborhoods. The same recruitment measures pertained to the B-Special force (this Class B of the Special constabulary were part-time, largely uncompensated volunteers), which supplemented the regular police, but which functioned with additional investigative and arrest authority after passage of the Special Powers Act to take on the characteristics of a Gestapo in the eyes of an oppressed minority.[39]

By the 1960s, when civil disobedience erupted in Northern Ireland cities, the economic picture of the province cast a dire prognosis for peace and harmony. Employment in the linen industry had fallen for half a decade and decreased 15 percent alone in the three years before 1955. In the 10-year period before 1965, the number of positions in plants employing 25 workers or more declined to 33,957 from 56,414. In shipbuilding, which accounted for one tenth of the province's manufacturing jobs, foreign competition from Japan and the continent cut the workforce 40 percent in Belfast from 1961 to 1964. In agriculture, employment fell to 28,000 workers, or by one third, from 1950 to 1960.[40] The economic malaise aggravated the communal tensions in what had became a de facto apartheid state, where Catholics and Protestants lived mainly in their own sections of the country

> *The economic malaise aggravated the communal tensions in what had became a de facto apartheid state, where Catholics and Protestants lived mainly in their own sections...*

or their own neighborhoods within urban centers. The Protestants formed the backbone of most of the business and professional classes, the skilled laborers, and largest farms. The Catholic residents, on the other hand, made up smaller farmers and the unskilled workers.

Commissioned by the Northern Ireland government, the Lord Cameron committee investigated and reported on the causes of the disturbances of the late 1960s. Among its chief findings, the committee emphasized "a rising sense of injustice and grievance among large sections of the Catholic population in public housing allocation, local government appointments, and manipulation of local elections against them."[41] Like contemporaneous events in the United States, these complaints had everything to do with civil rights and acceptance within the province and much less to do with the perennial "Republican" issues of Ulster's unification with the rest of Ireland or with resentment against the British crown. The comparison is not as farfetched as it might seem, for Northern Ireland's civil rights movements explicitly followed and modeled themselves on the American civil rights movements marching in Selma and Montgomery.

Catholic grievances also boiled over in the public housing arena. After World War II, Britain initiated public housing projects to address the pressing need for homes. By 1961, some 21 percent of all housing in Ulster was government built and rented to the province's residents. By 1971, the figure increased to 35 percent. But the expansion of publicly built residences only stepped up the complaints about the sectarian allocation of new homes, as Catholics found themselves on the short end of the housing stick in some districts. Local councils divvied up government-subsidized housing to ensure their electoral advantage.[42] With most of these councils controlled by Protestants, the distribution of government housing went to kith, kin, or other coreligious applicants.

Even greater under-representation of Catholics occurred in public employment. The overall sectarian representation for the allocation of employment in government-paid jobs appeared fair. The number of Catholics on the government payroll usually tracked with their percentage of the population, which in 1971 stood at 31 percent. But Protestants, or Unionists, were overrepresented in the higher grade positions. The Catholics filled the ranks with levels around 40 percent, slightly over their proportion of the entire population; but held only around 12–15 percent of the senior posts. Discrimination against Catholics ratcheted up in government-owned gas, electricity, and water industries. One study recorded that only 15 percent of the workers in those publicly owned services identified themselves as Catholic. Among the most senior government officials—such as MPs, top officials in local authorities, and high-level bureaucrats—only 11 percent professed Catholic identities.[43] It is impossible to escape the conclusions drawn from many reports and commissions that widespread discrimination existed in Northern Ireland prior to the Troubles.

Northern Ireland and the United States—Divided Societies

The societal divide in Northern Ireland paralleled American racial divisions that exploded in race riots inside U.S. urban centers during the 1960s. *Mutatis mutandis*, what was written in the 1968 Kerner Commission report after urban civil disorder hit American cities, "our nation is moving toward two societies, one black, one white—separate and unequal," can succinctly sum up Northern Ireland at the same time. Religion and culture defined polarity in Ulster, not ethnicity and skin pigmentation. But the divisions held similarities. The outrage and condemnation among the minority in Northern Ireland paralleled that in the African-American minority within the United States in the same period.

The Catholic community underwent changes beginning during the 1950s. Educated Catholics gravitated toward professions in teaching, medicine, and the legal professions because upper-level government jobs remained largely in Protestant hands. Foremost, they looked for ways to reform the political imbalances within Northern Ireland and to confront discriminatory practices in housing, jobs, and local governing bodies. To realize these goals, they formed political movements.

One particularly effective group was the Campaign for Social Justice (CSJ). The CSJ asserted that Nationalist politicians in parliaments in Westminster or Stormont were ineffective in attaining reforms. On the other hand, the CSJ also held that the violent tactics of the IRA during the 1950s were likely to fail by creating a backlash against Catholics. Like civil rights groups in the American South that also marched under the banner of "one man, one vote," the CSJ directed its attention at the central government, not local political councils. American civil rights groups wanted to involve the U.S federal government, and the CSJ sought to impact British public opinion rather than Unionist views, which it deemed impervious to reform. It contended that a Northern Ireland Parliament in the hands of the Unionist Party, which barred Catholics, had not given justice to the minority in the 40 years of its existence. Only British public opinion, if properly mobilized, could pressure Stormont for reform, since the British Parliament in Westminster held ultimate responsibility over the Ulster province.

Arrayed against Catholic groups pressing for reforms were Protestant movements determined to preserve the status quo, such as the Ulster Protestant Volunteers and the Ulster Constitution Defense Committee, led by the fiery churchman Ian Paisley. And behind these movements was the Ulster Volunteer Force (UVF) that fought against the IRA during the Anglo-Irish War. Both Catholic and Protestant populations contributed adherents to violent underground bands, which endorsed the use of force to attain political ends. Others joined overt groups to demonstrate publicly against their religious foes. Religion prevented the members of sectarian communities from joining anything but their own religious-based parties. The locked-in demographics and political alignments ruled out reforming society at the ballot box. Whereas majorities can usually acquiesce to the advancement of small minorities up the socioeconomic ladder, they recoil at larger minorities of around one third or more of the total population. The Protestant community in Northern Ireland fell into this category. And they protested Catholic demonstrations.

The "Troubles" Begin

What relighted the fuse in Northern Ireland was the emergence of public marches and protests by Catholic civil rights-type movements in the late 1960s. Modeled on their counterparts in the United States, the marchers and demonstrators courted television and print media attention as means to influence political decisions. If these activities got out of hand or produced Protestant counterdemonstrations, then disturbances, riots, and tense confrontations ensued. These standoffs did result in British governmental pressure on the Unionist-controlled government sitting in Stormont. Its mild reforms in response, nonetheless, fell short of the minority's demands, which embarked on more nonviolent civil disturbances. The anti-Unionist, however, did succeed in antagonizing Ulster's Unionist Party and its sympathizers such as Ian Paisley. Agitators on both sides shrunk the middle ground and sharpened the edginess in the streets.

Communal tensions came to a head when widespread rioting broke out in Northern Ireland in July 1969. After a month of sectarian strife, the Royal Ulster Constabulary (RUC), a police unit, nearly folded in exhaustion, and Stormont requested and received the deployment of British troops within the province to maintain order. From the Catholic minority viewpoint, the RUC lacked the impartiality of a neutral police force. To offset this Catholic distrust, the British subordinated the RUC to its military command. This arrangement caused a rivalry between the army and the RUC on the operational level until the late 1970s.

British troops stand guard in Falls Road, Belfast during rioting in August 1969 as a building burns in the background. Photo by permission of Newscom.

British authorities, more importantly, scrapped the auxiliary police force, the notorious B Specials, who were poorly trained reservist police. Neither police force had any Catholic officers, which left them open to charges of sectarian partiality, if not to deliberate violence against the minority. These were necessary but insufficient reforms because they did not go far enough. Nor did the minority see British soldiers as a particularly neutral party. In fact, the Irish government in Dublin called for United Nations' peacekeepers, who would be an impartial military to walk Northern Ireland's streets. The idea went nowhere because Britain sat on the United Nations Security Council. With the dispatch of the British Army to Ulster's streets, the Northern Ireland imbroglio was transformed from internal civil conflict to an intrastate peacekeeping mission that soon evolved into an insurgency. The Stormont government, in effect, lost its heretofore responsibility for managing the affairs in the now-volatile province.

At this pivotal point, Britain might have nipped the coming insurgency in the bud had it behaved with the forthcoming responsiveness of Washington administrations when faced with civil and racial unrest in several American cities during the late 1960s. The Westminster government did issue communiqués and set up commissions to address unfair housing and employment allocations. Britain's Labour government also laid the foundations for reconciliation policies. It secured passage of legislation through the Stormont parliament to address community relations, to prevent the incitement of hatred among religions in Northern Ireland, to centralize public-sector home building and allocation, and to transfer health services, water, sewage, and road building from local control to centralized allocation. These changes embodied efforts to streamline and rationalize delivery of public services as well as lay to rest the minorities' exclusion, which the British directly attributed to the rise in violence.

However, what followed soon thereafter was a backtracking from these early approaches due, in part, to the Conservative Party coming to power but also to developments in Ireland itself. The Provisional IRA's embrace of a physical-force strategy took the steam out of the reform strategy. Reformist packages appeared to be

> *The Provisional IRA's embrace of a physical-force strategy took the steam out of the reform strategy.*

rewarding bad behavior and disloyalty. The Protestant majority resented what it perceived as the appeasement and kid-glove treatment of violent culprits. Indeed, by the early 1970s, the emphasis shifted from carrying out the announced reforms to condemning the actions of "sinister elements or resurgent Republicanism that could not be satisfied by reform." [44]

London's security answer to rioting and disorder also struck the minority Catholic population as being partial to the Ulster Unionist. Rather than banning the provocative Orange parades and marches through the Catholic Bogside neighborhood in Belfast in summer 1970, the British authorities let them proceed. Additionally, the British Army imposed curfews and weapons searches exclusively in Catholic neighborhoods. Kicking in doors, ransacking of homes for weapons, humiliating automobile occupants in searches, rough questioning and harassment of pedestrians on the streets—all were heavy-handed practices initially employed as British troops rushed into Northern Ireland. The conduct alienated the Catholic population from the British authorities and ensured a steady stream of recruits to the Provisional IRAs. The vaunted British expertise in conducting sophisticated counterinsurgency measures was absent in Northern Ireland in the early 1970s.

Such actions forfeited neutrality and convinced Catholics that London's military was not in Northern Ireland to protect them. The British response, indeed, played into the hands of the Provisional IRA, which had begun sniping at Orange rioters and troops alike. By early 1971, British troops and RUC officers were being ambushed, machine-gunned, or bombed by a fierce underground movement. Catholic neighborhoods in Belfast erected barriers rendering them "no-go" areas to the crown's security forces. This also had the effect of denying the government intelligence about the insurgents.

The upsurge in civil disorder and the British government's military intervention reenergized and, at the same time, divided the hard-core Irish nationalist movements on both sides of the border between Ulster and the Irish Republic. Different objectives caused splits within the Irish Republican Army that saw itself as the heirs to the fighters in the 1919–1921 Irish War of Independence. Briefly, the so-called official IRA espoused a Marxist orientation and favored building a nonviolent and class-based alliance between Protestant and Catholic working classes in Northern Ireland to undermine the partition of Northern and Southern Ireland. This wing adopted early on some militant tactics, including shooting at British soldiers, for a short time before declaring an indefinite ceasefire in 1972. The traditional IRA believed that its violent campaign in the 1950s ended up failing because it alienated working-class people among Catholics and Protestants. It resolved not to repeat these tactics.

The so-called Provisional IRA (PIRA or "Provos") committed itself to never accepting partition of the island and to a violent national liberation front strategy against British and Protestant rule in Northern Ireland. Thus it harkened back to the Republicanism of the 1916 Easter Rebellion that fought for total expulsion of the British crown from all of Ireland. It drew support in the South as well as the North because of these historical roots. Like the official branch of the IRA, the "Provisionals" also made appeals to Ulster Protestants for a nonsectarian society with equal rights and opportunities for all religions. But the PIRA's advocacy of Republican ideals and use of violence completely turned off the Protestant majority. Instead, its message and means resonated with the Catholic population when faced with Protestant hooligan attacks on life, limb, and property. The PIRA picked up most of the old Republican networks in the North and recruited most of the militant youth who underwent radicalization with the 1969 riots. Yet the two wings of the IRA killed each other from time to time as their animus deepened. Similar splits took place within the Sinn Fein that mirrored the fissures between the armed cadres. Thus, there came into existence an "official" Sinn Fein and a "provisional" Sinn Fein. Other splinter factions later surfaced, staged attacks, and complicated the counterinsurgency response to spreading paramilitary violence.

Britain Responds on a Wider Scale

By summer 1971, the PIRA's shooting and bombing campaign reached an unprecedented level. By July, 55 people died violent deaths and another 600 suffered wounds within a population of only 1.5 million inhabitants. Some 320 shooting incidents and over 300 explosions occurred in the first six months of the year.

Demands for action prompted the Ulster government after consultation with Britain to strike back with a narrowly effective but widely controversial policy of internment without trial of suspected insurgents in Catholic areas. The Ulster officials convinced London authorities that no organized terrorist networks existed within the Protestant community. Therefore, the British concentrated on the Catholics. On 9 August 1971, the British Army staged a series of dawn raids to arrest 450 suspects; it actually netted 342 men, with almost 100 immediately released. Of those still held, many had little or no connection to the IRA.[45]

As a backlash to the internment policy, Northern Ireland's towns exploded in killings, burnings, and displacement of residents, leaving 2,000 Protestants and 7,000 Catholics homeless. Refugee camps south of the border accommodated some 2,500 fleeing Catholics. There were over 100 fatalities and several hundred injured. Soon allegations of "ill-treatment" arose from the arrested prisoners, who contended that detainees endured "in-depth" interrogations while hooded, forced to stand for long periods, and deprived of sleep. The immediate consequences of the tougher approach backfired on the officials.

Internment and harsh interrogations caused a jump in PIRA numbers. Official IRA units went over to the "Provisionals," and new recruits flocked to the underground movement. Internment also occasioned a change in PIRA operations. It widened its target list, homing in on Protestant-owned factories, shops, working-class pubs, and other economic facilities. It also zeroed in on the RUC and the Ulster Defense Regiment by assassinating its members whether unarmed, uniformed, or off duty as well as when they manned their posts. Even worse, internment led moderate and cooperative

Catholic politicians, officials, and prominent figures to resign their positions or withdraw their cross-sectarian participation. In their eyes, British actions did nothing but defend the Unionist power and privilege in Northern Ireland.

Finally, Catholic reactions to internment sparked a counter-reaction among the Protestant community. Disparate Protestant vigilantes and paramilitary formations merged into the Ulster Defense Association in autumn 1971. Like the older Ulster Volunteer Force, the UDA settled on the term "loyalist" rather than "unionist" to identify their cause; but the two are used interchangeably despite the confusion for the unfamiliar observer. They were loyal to the connection with Britain and prided themselves on allegiance to the crown and the Union Jack. The UDA membership reached over 40,000 at its peak in 1972, but the bulk of membership held full-time day jobs. The UDA and the UVF usually rallied for marches or to the barricades in defensive roles. A hard core, however, moved beyond Protestant mob violence to solo revenge murders, often carried out randomly against uninvolved Catholics walking home from work or a pub. In short, the internment policy deepened the Troubles as Northern Ireland spiraled into widespread sectarian bloodshed.

Worse, much worse, arose. The joint Stormont-Westminster alliance reached a watershed in the wake of the notorious Bloody Sunday incident on 30 January 1972. As demonstrators from a banned civil rights march in Derry descended into a melee, British troops used rubber bullets and water cannons to contain rowdy youths. In the chaotic scene, the storied Parachute Regiment reportedly responded to sounds of gunfire with its own rifle shots. When the firing stopped, 13 civil-

Demonstrators and British troops face each other on Bloody Sunday, 30 January 1972. Photo by permission of Newscom.

ians lay dead (an additional one died later) and 17 suffered bullet wounds. Controversy still swirls around whether the fault for the shootings lies with the paratroopers or members of the Official IRA, who may have first fired on the "paras." Bloody Sunday galvanized fierce anti-British emotions within the Catholic community on both sides of the Irish border. In Dublin to the south, rioters burned the British embassy. In Northern Ireland, a wave of bombings killed and maimed shoppers and restaurant-goers. Violence spread to Britain itself where Irish bombers detonated explosions near the barracks of the Parachute Regiment, killing 7 civilians. In all, 467 people died in 1972, the worst year of the Troubles.

When the Westminster government, in response to the violent contagion, demanded that the Stormont Parliament turn over control of the local security forces to British authority, the parliamentary body refused in spite of its inability to halt the rising tide of attacks. Then, Prime Minister Edward Heath suspended the Northern Ireland government in March 1972 initially for one year but as it turned out for over two decades. Britain decided to govern directly the unruly province and vested Ulster's powers in a newly created Secretary of State for Northern Ireland. This meant that Britain could implement policies unfiltered by the political establishment in Ulster. It is little commented on, but the new dispensation also subordinated all the security forces to British governmental control, meaning political ends trumped strictly military measures. In short, Britain's direct rule of the chaotic Six Counties resulted in a quasi-colonial form of government, which London attempted to balance with a Northern Ireland advisory council to provide input on local matters. Direct British rule brought no end in the violence, however. Other more imaginative steps were needed.

The antidotes to the virus of insurgency proved to be powerful society-altering measures, which have too often gone unappreciated—or under appreciated—by soldiers and students of counterinsurgency, who became mesmerized by the facile techniques of counterinsurgency. These proponents or observers saw the surface tactics of the British Army patrolling in small units on foot, donned in soft berets (not helmets), or riding in opened top vehicles (not buttoned-down tanks). They missed the vastly deeper and broader societal reordering and diplomatic forays that transformed the nature of the insurgency and delivered peace.

Terrorism and Response

For 20 years a low-intensity conflict washed over Ulster, occasionally spilling into the Republic of Ireland and the United Kingdom. More than 3,600 people died from political violence in Northern Ireland from 1969 and 1998. To confront the escalating violence, London fielded more security personnel to the peak amount of 30,000 in 1972—a time of spiked violence. It should be noted that the ranks of Britain's security personnel included officers from the homegrown RUC and Ulster Defense Regiment (that replaced the notorious B Specials). Gradually as conditions permitted, London scaled down its security presence. At the time of the IRA ceasefire in 1994, the declining troop level reached 17,000. By mid-2007, only some 5,000 British troops remained garrisoned in province. By most accounts, the insurgent numbered less than 500 at one time and at their peak.[46]

Much has been written about British military techniques utilized to combat bombings, sniping, and assassinations. The bulk of the assessments have stressed the changeover in tactics from a heavy-handed, clumsy, rigid militarized occupation to a deft, agile, intelligence-informed unconventional force. Known as the "soft approach," the British strategy gradually centered on nonaggressive reactions to attacks. It emphasized interaction with the locals to present a nonthreatening posture and to tease out intelligence. British officers touted this stability-by-civility course of action. Rather than the "full-battle rattle" of other counterinsurgency armies, such as the U.S. military, small British foot patrols wore the soft beret, not weighty Kevlar helmets and bulky full-body armor. They patrolled on foot, not in vehicles. British authorities have not been shy in advocating these procedures over the years to their American counterparts. Even advisability of removing sunglasses when talking with Iraqis was held up as British virtue.

In the course of the Iraq insurgency, British officers were free with advice for "shoulder-holster wearing" American generals with a "strong streak of Hollywood" to emulate the behavior of Britain's servicemen who "were undemonstrative, phlegmatic, and pragmatic."[47] Much of this tactical-level advice proved to be on target, such as dialing down an over reliance on heavy firepower in crowded streets, stepping up thorough intelligence gathering with up-to-the minute analysis, and turning to community-based policing methods rather than conventional attritional warfare in build-up areas that redounded against a liberating occupation force.

Among the advertised British success stories, Northern Ireland usually stood near the top. It was in the rainy climes of the Ulster pocket that the British Army touted one of its counterinsurgency triumphs. Knowledgeable officers pointed out specific British units and lessons to their American counterparts. Britain's 14 Intelligence Company enlisted informers as well as inserted bugging and tracing equipment in intelligence-gathering operations. The elite Special Air Service (SAS) used with great affect wiretapping, night-vision equipment, massive surveillance of suspects, and the high-velocity bullet, rather than wide-radius explosives, to dispatch a single terrorist. The SAS formed a "symbiotic relationship" for tip-offs with RUC's Special Branch, which possessed a network of informers in the Catholic community.[48]

The SAS's lethal zeroing in on IRA operatives with deadly force resulted in the insurgents labeling it the "Special Assassination Squad" out of fear. Its methods did much to curb terrorism in Six Counties, but they were not without controversy. Even SAS officers were said to have backed a shoot-to-kill policy, although units did take prisoners on occasion. SAS troops killed some 28 IRA members from 1987–1992 in ambushes and assaults.[49] Moreover, a SAS hit team gunned down three unarmed IRA operatives on the streets of Gibraltar in 1988—an incident that set off a firestorm of controversy in the European press. The SAS's lethality did undercut the avowed governmental policy of "police primacy" while it strove to keep the lid on IRA attacks.

The SAS record combined with other less deadly counterinsurgency practices contributed to the British Army's reputation for winning low-intensity conflicts. These methods established the British Army's place within the pantheon of victories over guerrillas and terrorists.[50] John Keegan, the British military historian, wrote: "Irish Republicans hate those they call 'Crown forces' for their professionalism, since it blocked their ambition to control the Northern Irish cities themselves."[51]

In Northern Ireland, one British officer noted: "It is doubtful whether any other Army could have coped without resorting to massive retaliation."[52] Indeed, British troops behaved with remarkable restraint after the Bloody Sunday incident. While civilian casualties made up the bulk of the more than 3,600 killed, British Army casualties soared three to one over paramilitary deaths, at about 1,000 security personnel to 300 insurgents killed. Of the security forces, two thirds of their deaths came from the ranks of local personnel from 1976 to 1990, compared with one third from 1971–1975.[53] Rather than heavy retaliation for lost security forces, the British authorities practiced restraint and precisely targeted strike backs against individual PIRA members. Thus the same British officer-author writing in 1985 reported: "During the [first] 16 years of the Emergency, the Security Forces have reduced violence and the potential of the IRA to achieve damage, disruption and destruction, to a degree that in the dark days of the early 1970s often seemed impossible."[54]

Even the noted military author Martin Van Creveld bought into "the real secret behind the British success: extreme self-control." The Israeli expert added: "Whatever else might happen, the British did not allow themselves to be provoked. . . By showing restraint, the British did not alienate people other than those who were already fighting them."[55] How this "reduced violence" came about was due not just to Army restraint, skill, and doggedness but also to political actions to lessen the economic and political marginalization of the Catholic minority, as this essay seeks to demonstrate.

Patience ranks near the top of qualities for counterinsurgency, but it is trumped by political action. Restraint could make the Army no enemies, but it also could make it no friends; jobs, housing, and education programs could win over the uncommitted to grudging acquiescence of continued British rule. It is an established fact that the British governments were not only able to adapt the military COIN measures; they changed their policy prescriptions too. This essay is focused on the political steps that secured peace in Northern Ireland. But it should, briefly, acknowledge the purely martial counterinsurgency formula for stabilization. These include urban foot patrols, painstaking and frustrating surveillance of suspects, instant checkpoints or reactions to incidents, bomb-disposal methods, redundant radio networks to maintain communications in a crisis, improved searching techniques, and, most important, enhanced intelligence gathering.

The British also stepped away from much overt patrolling in early stages of the insurgency to more covert operations by the mid-1980s as more effective to combat the terrorists' element of surprise. Fewer troops on the streets also meant a less intrusive reminder of the British presence. When the IRA shed its battalion-size organization for cellular structure to elude detection, it required the British to also adapt with the four-man "brick" as the standard patrol unit. The IRA cell apparatus also necessitated greater reliance on police work and intelligence to combat the dispersed network. The most controversial British approach involved the use of the Protestant or loyalists paramilitaries. This policy included more than just passing intelligence to British handlers; it sometimes meant loyalist bombings of Catholic pubs or assassination of Catholics alleged to be IRA members in a sectarian "dirty war."[56] British forces and the loyalist gangs shared the mutual goal of eliminating the IRA. The collaboration may have helped facilitate the containment of PIRA violence, but it allowed the paramilitaries to depict the British forces as little more than allies of the Protestants.

The lethal-force incidents by both sides did, in fact, first taper off and then end completely. The debate, however, centers on the cause of the decline in the killings and maiming. Too many thoughtless writers, analysts, and simply pundits credit the tactical-level COIN steps almost exclusively or at the least overemphasize them in their findings. Standard military accounts emphasize the success of tactics, while making little, if any, mention of civic-action measures. For example, one book series on the history, organization, and equipment of famous fighting forces that soldiers would be inclined to read actually proposed: "The Security Forces [in Northern Ireland] estimate that through a combination of their overt patrolling and undercover intelligence-gathering operations they prevent more than two thirds of all planned terrorist attacks." Without explanation, this author went on to note: "Each year the level of PIRA activity drops and its support in the Catholic community is gradually reduced."[57] The reader concludes wrongly that military operations alone achieved a containment of terrorism. There is no mention of other factors, such as political reconciliation measures, improved socio-economic conditions, or diplomatic accommodations with the Republic of Ireland to the south.

The Arsenal of Victory: Local Government, Jobs, Houses, and Education

Britain's nonmilitary responses to the paramilitary violence played *the* major role in the eventual pacification, far outweighing the counter-insurgency measures of small-unit foot patrols, intelligence gathering, and minimal use of force. Whereas in Iraq and Afghanistan, the U.S. Army and Marines carry out—or at least ensure—the bulk of the civic action type programs among the populations, in Northern Ireland the British civilian authorities took responsibility for such "hearts and minds" programs.

Early on, the British government implemented some remedial programs to address long-standing grievances within Northern Ireland that contributed to the PIRA's insurgency against Britain's governance. Catholics had long felt disadvantaged and discriminated against in jobs, housing, and education compared to the non-Catholic population. Their sense of exclusion from societal amenities fueled their support for the PIRA with a pool of recruits, a ready-made intelligence network, safe houses, and financial or human resources. By lessening Catholic alienation and anger, the British authorities banked on separating the bulk of this non-Protestant population from radical members who directly enabled the PIRA insurgency.

Once Britain suspended the Stormont Parliament and directly ruled Northern Ireland, it correctly identified the long-term solution to the Troubles as social reform. It also reduced the number of British troops by 6,000 from its 1972 levels at the end of 1976. London directed the political process and allocation of resources to the beleaguered enclave. In the decade following direct rule, public spending drastically increased. Social security outlays for example spiked by 102 percent to cope with the rise in unemployment, violence, and underdevelopment.

How the London government dealt with violence emanating from Protestants will be covered below in the Community Relations and Education section. Suffice here to note that the Protestant majority—who often benefited more than the Catholic minority from access to public housing, jobs, and education—concentrated on their established alliance with the United Kingdom. Once the Protestant community realized that it would not be abandoned to any scheme to enfold the Ulster province within the rest of Ireland, they generally moved away from attacks on British security forces. Protestant gunmen did kill Catholics in revenge killings, which kept Northern Ireland in turmoil. But generally the London government identified Catholics for their social service enticements, although Protestants also benefited indirectly by the rise in prosperity and government benefits. One illustration of Britain's spiraling outlays in the embattled province was the noteworthy growth in retirement pensions, unemployment benefits, and healthcare benefits, which jumped to £257,458,000 (approximately 772,374,000 in 1980 U.S. dollars) in 1978 from £66,129,000 (about 198,387,000 in 1980 U.S. dollars) in 1969, nearly a fourfold increase.[58]

The Provisional IRA and other murderous gangs drew their recruits from working-class Catholics, the most aggrieved cross-section of the minority. Others within the Catholic community preferred the nonviolent approach of the Social Democratic and Labour Party, one of the constitutional parties of Northern Ireland that contested elections and held seats in the Stormont parliament. British civilian officials strove to drain away manpower, intelligence, and financing from the paramilitaries, while trying to channel disgruntled members of the minority into recognized political parties to resolve their grievances and attain their goals. Hence, London devoted attention and money to three major sectors in Northern Ireland society—jobs, housing, and education. Each will be briefly analyzed.

Local Government Reform

It took longer than anticipated to reform local government after the imposition of direct rule, but in spring 1973 the first District Council elections were held under revised procedures. These reformed provisions provided new boundaries for the District Councils, voting systems, and enfranchisement. A return to proportional representation, which had been scrapped in 1929 to ensure Protestant political victories in local, provincial, and Westminster elections through the gerrymandering of voting districts, enabled the Catholic minority parties to win more seats than under the old discriminatory system. This reform thus brought more Catholic representation to District Councils, which held resources and powers over employment in government service jobs.

The election returns in 26 District Councils led to minority views and votes. In the first election after the reforms, the Unionist Party (Protestant) had a clear majority on only one District Council. For their part, the main Catholic parties controlled no single Council. This outcome, nevertheless, built in a healthy give-and-take process among Council members, who now had to form voting coalitions to pass bills, allocate resources, and accomplish agendas. In short, the minority views and concerns now counted in the negotiations in ways unheard of before the British reforms. The hegemony of the Unionist Party, therefore, suffered a setback. Like any political reform, this one had drawbacks in that it led not to immediate political miracles, since sectarianism did not suddenly evaporate. Yet, Catholic politicians for the first time in 44 years sensed an elevation in their participation in local government and decision-making. Therefore, the political structure underwent a substantial overhaul.[59]

Along with local governmental reforms, various London governments attempted to bring province-wide political parties to the negotiating table. In fact, there were even talks with the PIRA representatives that punctuated truces between paramilitary and British security forces. Mainly, however, London sought to engage the so-called constitutional parties in discussions about the devolution of its power back to Northern Ireland. These British initiatives often failed abjectly, as Catholic and Protestant parties boycotted the talks or presented programs irreconcilable with those of other parties, leading to complete breakdowns in negotiations. Some wanted one legislature; others favored two. Catholic leaders wanted integration into the Republic of Ireland. Protestant politicians favored complete incorporation of Ulster within the United Kingdom. How the control of the security forces would be divvied up plagued the talks. In short, there was little or no consensus among the parties. But an electoral process presented an alternative to the bomb and bullet. Over time, this political approach took hold and led to the end of sectarian violence in the province.

One unforeseen political development of enormous import grew out of the election of imprisoned PIRA members to representative bodies in the early 1980s. Bobby Sands, one of ten incarcerated and self-martyring PIRA men, led a hunger strike that turned out to be a propaganda coup. Before his death from self-inflicted starvation, Sands won a by-election (special election) for a vacant seat in the Westminster Parliament. Two other PIRA prisoners won election to the Republic of Ireland's parliament in Dublin. If imprisoned PIRA militants could win elections from prisons, then a political strategy, rather than a likely fruitless terrorist campaign, might attain the political ends for which the Catholic rebels so desperately and menacingly bombed and assassinated. This realization—made possible in part by the reforms—dawned on Gerry Adams, the Sinn Fein leader, and orientated him toward a political settlement that took 15 years to come to fruition. Britain's openness to political reform and acceptance of its sworn enemies to election victories displayed a strategic flexibility. There are even hints that British officials intrigued in IRA politics to bring about a faction favoring elections and a political resolution.[60] Be that as it may, Sinn Fein went on to be the largest party in Northern Ireland and won seats in Westminster, Dublin, Belfast, and the European Parliament by the early 21st century.

Housing for the Minority

Government, or public, housing assumes a greater portion of dwellings in Northern Ireland than in the United States where the private sector, aside from city or federally built inner-city residences, dominates. Some of this government intervention is an outgrowth of socialist-style governments across the Atlantic, and some stems from the rebuilding of destroyed housing stock during World War II. By 1971, some 35 percent of the homes in Northern Ireland were public-rented accommodations. British governments supplied funds for housing construction, but it never met demands. Shortages of homes still existed throughout the province before and during the Troubles.

This expansion of the government's role in home building led to fresh charges of discrimination, for many newly constructed homes went to Protestants. Not all areas of Northern Ireland witnessed housing allocation unfair to the Catholic minority, but enough instances took place to cause a sense of grievance that found its confirmation in other forms of sectarian-based denial.

It was, in fact, the discriminatory allocation of housing by local authorities that spurred the civil rights protests in the late 1960s. Local councils, as indicated above, worked to gather Protestant voters in their districts and confine Catholics in their segregated neighborhoods. This segregation policy also locked in Protestant residents nearer to employment opportunities. Thus the overall practice reproduced Unionist-controlled local councils in a form of a residential apartheid. At the start of the Troubles, the London government established a centralized authority, the Northern Ireland Housing Executive (NIHE), in place of existing bodies and the 67 local authorities. Like other service boards in health, education, and libraries, the NIHE embodied the mission of eliminating the grounds for complaints in order to reduce the basis of underlying disaffection "behind violence and ensure future viability and well-being."[61]

Under the NIHE's auspices, housing starts initially spurted to over 9,000 homes in 1971, two years after its startup, but then declined to only 4,000 units three years later before it leaped again to over 9,000 in 1976. This uneven production curve was traceable to changes from a Labour to a Conservative government in London and to civil disorder within Northern Ireland. Sentiments in Northern Ireland and the United Kingdom also impacted British policies. Protestants and others believed that government rewards to Catholic home-seekers, in effect, were little more than pandering to those guilty of perpetuating violence. Consequently, London's housing and other "hearts and minds" projects were prey to fluctuations induced by the outlook of politicians and their constituents.

But even the coming to power of the Conservatives in 1979, who were philosophically opposed to the expansion of the role of government in housing, saw another aberration in the usual policy of the governing party. Unexpectedly, the Conservatives spared cuts in housing expenditures in Northern Ireland that hit the rest of the United Kingdom. Two years later, in fact, the *per capita* housing expenditure in the Six Counties stood at almost four times the amount in England and Wales.[62] This departure in Conservative principles prudently came about for the practical matter of reducing Catholic bitterness, not an overall change in views.

A unique institution, the NIHE became the United Kingdom's first comprehensive housing authority. In addition to government funds, it gained money from rental income and sales of homes. From its founding until 2001, it "built over 80,000 new homes, housed more than 500,000 people, improved 350,000 homes in the private sector, sold over 90,000 homes to sitting tenants."[63] The sheer breadth of its housing activities had a substantial impact on making more homes and rentals available in Northern Ireland, thereby dramatically impacting the availability of living accommodations to Catholics and Protestants alike.

Employment for the Discriminated

Employment discrimination constituted another sector that caused hostile feelings of inequality through barriers that disadvantaged the Catholic minority. These inequalities smacked of religious bias in both public and private sectors. Among government jobs, the Catholic job-holders occupied positions commensurate with their percentage of the population, according to independent studies. But discrepancies appeared in higher level positions, where Protestants filled senior posts in numbers disproportionate to their province-wide numbers. Top civil servants, however, argued that Catholics lacked the education standards for the uppermost slots or they simply did not apply for them. Nongovernment job prospects presented another dismal picture. In the private sector, Catholic workers usually held the manual laboring jobs, while Protestants occupied the managerial or executive positions.

Compounding the disturbing employment portrait was the overall worsening of Northern Ireland's economy. Foreign competition eroded the province's once-prosperous shipbuilding and textile industries. So British efforts to alleviate unfairness in the workplace had also to concentrate on spurring overall economic development. London established the Local Enterprise Development Unit in 1971 to direct aid toward small firms in rural districts to expand manufacturing plants. Two other agencies replaced it, each with a broadened mandate and funds to stimulate industrial development.

Later in 1982, Britain replaced these agencies with the Industrial Development Board that embraced several functions to revitalize industries, transfer technology, and increase production. All these efforts, and others, aimed to alleviate unemployment, which hovered around 14 percent compared with 10 in the rest of the United Kingdom by the 1990s. Earlier unemployment figures in shipbuilding, agriculture, and textile manufacturing pushed into the 50 percent range as these traditional industries collapsed in the face of foreign competition. These precipitous declines fed Catholic perceptions of job discrimination, although non-Catholics suffered as well. But still Catholic workers fared worse, being 2.6 times more likely to be jobless.[64] The labor problems, therefore, contributed to the insurgency. And the beginnings of the insurgency only deepened the economic plight and worsened employment figures in a vicious cycle downward.

To combat employment discrimination, the British government established the Fair Employment Agency in 1976. Its investigations revealed that in civil service, banking, universities, and large engineering companies, a disproportionate number of Protestants were hired, pointing toward a pattern of discrimination. It determined that employers must provide equality of opportunity to the minority population. Next, it set up regulations, not unlike the affirmative action programs in the United States aimed at getting African Americans into the workplace, which pressured employers to attain a sectarian balance. The Fair Employment Act imposed no formal quotas, but it strengthened the Fair Employment Commission, which oversaw hiring practices. The act and the commission made discrimination unacceptable among employers by requiring employers to monitor the composition of their workforce.[65]

Even Conservatives, when they took power again at Westminster in 1979, recognized the necessity of financial subsidy of private industrial development along with public-sector industries. Because Conservatives are not wont to lavish taxpayer funds on public work schemes, their turnaround is proof that they recognized the need to address violence across the Irish Sea. The high degree of their support to government funding for Northern Ireland's dismal unemployment problem differed in lower amounts for outlays in England, Scotland, and Wales because of the overriding security threat posed by IRA attacks. Conservative MPs funded the declining manufacturing sector but also moved to embrace the new technology sector and service sector, as ultimately a better bet to lessen unemployment in the province. Despite all government funds during the 1980s, unemployment remained in the double-digit percentiles because of the accelerated decline of Northern Ireland shipbuilding and manufacturing industries.[66]

Progress in changing the discriminatory pattern against Catholic workers was slow but an unmistakable and steady improvement took place. The Fair Employment Commission reported in 1995 that the gap between Catholic and Protestant employment had been narrowed in the private sector, although the minority still lagged. Catholics were still two times as likely to be unemployed. But the Catholic portion of the work force had narrowly expanded by 2 percent from 1990 to 1996.[67]

However, in the public sector of employment, where direct British rule held much more sway over hiring, Catholic employment leapt ahead of the pre-Troubles period. What facilitated the increased participation of the minority in civil service jobs was vast expansion of that workforce. The British transferred social services from local districts, and largely Protestant control, to an array of agencies, such as the newly formed Housing Executive, health and personal services, education and library boards, and other civil service functions. Only 12,000 people worked in Northern Ireland's government sector at the end of the 1960s. In 1991, the expanded civil service apparatus employed over 50,000 Catholic workers, which constituted 36 percent of the entire government employment (excluding security forces)—a percentage commensurate with the size of Northern Ireland's Catholic population. Catholic representation in the senior-most positions still lagged at 24 percent, but it amounted to a significant rise over the past two decades.[68]

The enlargement of the public sector and consequent expansion in employment produced a stabilizing effect. But this surge in government jobs resulted in an economic downside over time. By the early 21st century, it became recognized in the Ulster province that big government with its large bureaucracy could place a drag on future economic growth in the private sector.[69] Still, there are few detractors of the overall approach.

Household income for the entire Ulster province rose during the two decades to figures comparable to those in Scotland and Wales, although less than in England itself.[70] Once again, however, Catholic households under-performed Protestant families in overall income but with smaller disparities than during the 1960s. Women's employment also underwent fundamental shifts as the female proportion of workers went to 48 percent in the 1990s from 36 percent in the early 1950s, with particular employment gains for married women. Creating jobs for Catholics and Protestants alike put people to work and lessened intersectarian tension. Unemployment, the bane of Northern Ireland's economy for a decade, greatly lessened. At its peak of 17 percent in 1986, the unemployment rate fell steadily to 5.7 percent in 2002, which compared favorably with the average 8.4 percent in the European Union, though it was still high by American standards.[71] With jobs and income, the average person's life improved, reducing the drift toward sectarian conflict.

Spending on job creation came also from the International Fund for Ireland, an independent organization established by the British and Irish government in 1986. Funding came from those two countries along with the United States, European Union, Australia, Canada, and New Zealand. By 2001, Washington alone had donated $100 million to the International Fund of Ireland. In 2008 the total gifts over the years reaches over $1 billion. The International Fund concentrated on the Six Counties and the five counties located in Ireland that bordered Northern Ireland. Millions of dollars were raised and expended to build business and employ people. President Bill Clinton's representative to the International Fund, James Lyons, stated during his tenure from 1993 to 2001, that the organization put about 20,000 people to work and funded some 400 projects. Lyons also concentrated on expanding small businesses like auto mechanics, beauty parlors, and housing-remodeling firms. The International Fund also worked to invigorate community colleges and vocational training.[72] By the early 21st century, Northern Ireland's economy, while still fragile, had demonstrated rising prosperity, falling unemployment, and reduced emigration from the province.

Community Relations and Education

Another crucial initiative to facilitate intersectarian reconciliation lay in the British government's intervention into the community relations arena. This activity is less quantifiable than employment figures and income levels but equally important to social harmony among bitterly and deeply divided groups. The cynical might view these projects as too "warm and fuzzy" for real soldiers, but in reality they represent another front in the "hearts and minds" campaign. Not unlike similar policies in the United States to break down interracial stereotypes, Britain set out to step up contacts between Catholics and Protestants, who often lived in near-apartheid separation, to foster tolerance and cultural pluralism. It also clearly announced its policies of nurturing equal opportunity for all Northern Ireland's citizens. To institutionalize these policies, it established an agency within the office of the Secretary of Northern Ireland, Britain's key political figure in the province. Three years later in 1990, it formed a Northern Ireland Community Relations Council (NICRC). That same year witnessed the passage of legislation for educational reforms, which will be addressed below.

It must be emphasized that the official community relations efforts built on many nongovernmental initiatives dating from early 1960. These private contacts among groups expanded at the end of that decade with the onset of rioting and intercommunal attacks. These reconciliation groups pioneered techniques and influenced school education and youth work programs. Many of the lessons from nongovernmental organizations (NGOs) were incorporated into official bodies like the NICRC. The British officials, for example, instituted proposals for police accountability to the community and transferred other NGO experiences to educational institutions. The central government borrowed, amplified, and instituted policies to foster social harmony. It conducted audits of government agencies for compliance with mutual tolerance measures. It appointed community relations officers for each of the province's 26 local districts, promoted intercommunity contact projects, created intersectarian youth service agencies, and installed antisectarian and antidiscrimination programs with the trade unions.[73]

Hesitantly, the British government also ventured into the educational system in Northern Ireland. Again, individuals and private organizations preceded governmental policy and provided a foundation for official steps.

In 1982, a decade after teachers and academicians advocated curriculum changes to enhance tolerance, the authorities produced a circular entitled *The Improvement of Community Relations: The Contribution of Schools*, which argued that teachers and administrators have "a responsibility for helping children learn to understand and respect each other."[74] After this initial effort, the government, seven years later, issued the Education Reform (Northern Ireland) Order, which specified "education for mutual understanding."[75] These tentative steps paved the way for a more dramatic departure in official educational policy.

The British government inaugurated religiously integrated schools, which enrolled about equal numbers of Catholic and Protestant children. Three years later, in 1993, the government operated 17 primary and 4 post-primary schools with some 3,500 pupils—which made up just 1 percent of the school-aged population. Despite the tiny attendance, the government's initiative traveled uncharted territory in the sharply sectarian landscape of Northern Ireland, where Catholic- and Protestant-dominated schools were an integral part of Northern Ireland life.

Accessibility to higher education for Northern Irish teens figured prominently in London's pacification policies. Teenagers enrolled in university or vocational schools learned a profession or trade, which led to hope for gainful employment, rather than to the terrorist cells. Having been barred or restricted from post-secondary schooling or training for decades, Catholic,

Teenagers enrolled in university or vocational schools learned a profession or trade, which led to hope for gainful employment, rather than to the terrorist cells.

as well as Protestant, youth enjoyed greater entry to education after the Troubles began and the British governments removed hurdles by providing monies. For example, grants to Northern Ireland's universities increased to £31,357,000 (approximately 94,071,000 in 1981 dollars) in 1981 from £15,126,000 (approximately 45,378,000 in 1981 U.S. dollars) in 1978, thus nearly doubling funding.[76] Total university full-time students increased by 75 percent overall and doubled for women attendees from 1966 to 1975.[77]

Along with the well-established premier higher education institutions such as Queen's University and the University of Ulster, the Open University expanded university places for residents. Established in 1971, Open University, a United Kingdom-wide college, functioned somewhat like American community colleges. The majority of the students attended part time and tended to be in their mid-20s rather than in their late teens.

It is unique within the British educational system in that it has no entry requirements, making it accessible to students without mainstream university requirements. Thus, it appealed to young people wishing to better their present employment with more education.

Vocational training jumped substantially for males and females after the start of British direct rule. A sampling of figures demonstrates the swelling of students enrolled in vocational training, while the overall population remained static. The numbers of male students shot up to 22,366 in nonadvance programs in 1980 from 18,342 in 1974. Women's enrollment saw a corresponding increase to 19,597 students in nonadvance programs in 1980 from 14,170 in 1974.[78] Along with educational outlays, health services also witnessed far more government attention.

Government expenditures for health services in Northern Ireland more than doubled in the early 1980s from those in the late 1970s. Total outlays to hospitals, general medical services, and health administration went to £409,243,000 (approximately 1,227,729,000 in 1980 U.S. dollars) in 1981 from £202, 400,000 (approximately 607,200,000 in 1980 U.S. dollars).[79]

By the mid-1990s, it became an accepted fact that government investments in housing, education, and job programs had tilted heavily toward Catholic areas because British officials believed that long neglect of the minority had bred the problems for law and order. London attention alleviated some of the Catholics' smoldering resentments, which contributed to the tamping down of PIRA attacks—the goal of its economic and political programs. London's approach, on the other hand, disgruntled Protestant loyalists, who felt betrayed by the object of their allegiance. The pro-British Ulsterites dissented from what they viewed as concessions, rewarding Republican violence. They rankled at the too-soft approach by the RUC, which under its new dispensation tried to be a nonaligned police force by recruiting Catholic officers.

British civilian officials sought to reassure the Protestant majority through political statements and actions. The bulk of the non-Catholic population warily greeted London's assurances. A fringe element, however, took vengeance against PIRA killings. Protestant vigilante-type paramilitaries matched, and even exceeded, PIRA attacks by targeting republican activists or randomly killing Catholics. One Protestant politician—John Taylor, then the deputy leader of the Ulster Unionists—attributed the PIRA's ending its insurgency to loyalists' killings. Taylor held that loyalist paramilitaries had "begun to overtake the IRA as being the major paramilitary and terrorist organization in Northern Ireland."[80] With the prospect of further sectarian warfare and a welcome political and economic change by the British government, the PIRA declared victory and decided to make peace.

In the end, London's policies constituted a balancing act to alleviate Catholic animosity and alienation without incurring Protestant disaffection and backlash. The peace and stability enjoyed in Northern Ireland during the past decade indicate a qualified success for British civilian governments' approach. The Six Counties at the least entered a new chapter in their history and in London's relations with the province. History never stands still and the political gains could still be disrupted as Ulster is capable of sliding backwards. Yet, each passing year of peace affirms the correctness of the path taken by London governments.

Diplomacy

British policy in Northern Ireland became a focal point for media scrutiny. Like America's contemporaneous war in Vietnam, Britain's handling of the conflict in Ulster received abundant print and television reportage and commentary. British governments therefore operated with an eye to the international press corps' coverage. The public relations aspects of policies and actions often framed the parameters of discussion and planning phases of its actions. Besides, with a cherished political culture of liberal democracy, Britain was precluded from adopting extreme measures, such as those implemented by Argentinian authorities in the "disappearances" of political opponents during the 1970s. A South American military dictatorship might be able temporarily to carry out a "dirty war" against its dissidents, but a well-established democracy and with extensive international relationships could not do so.

Although the international media had to be taken into account by London in its responses to IRA attacks, its impact was not just some distant and vague concern that might be managed by clever spin operations on the world stage. Events within the northern Six Counties and their media reportage cast a direct spell over London's most important international partner—the Republic of Ireland—in the Six Counties crisis. Sharing an ill-defined border with the Ulster province, the Republic loomed as the most crucial foreign determinate of events in Northern Ireland. True enough, Irish-Americans in the United States and their partisans in elected office exercised political leverage from time to time over British politicians. Some even clandestinely funneled money that purchased IRA arms. Nevertheless, Americans of Irish descent never constituted the key outside variable in Britain's calculations. The Irish Republic did.

Defeating terrorism depended upon the greater Ireland's cooperation in cross-border security and extradition of suspected gunmen. The Irish public and their governments were mightily affected by Britain's handling of their Catholic brethren on the northeastern shoulder of the island to a much greater degree than Irish Americans. Therefore they scrutinized and agonized over British policy and behavior in Northern Ireland. Quite simply, British goals in Northern Ireland hinged disproportionately on productive relations with Ireland. As a consequence, London had to forge cooperative relations with Dublin or watch the Republic of Ireland become a permanent insurgent sanctuary.

The Republic of Ireland and Britain established a Joint Law Enforcement Commission, composed of members of the judiciary from both countries in 1974, to sort out the disputes occasioned by suspected terrorists claiming political status in the Republic to escape extradition from the South. It should come as no surprise to observers of international law and legal disputes that the commission disagreed among itself, and its recommendations encountered determined opposition in Dublin and London. Surrendering sovereignty either by extraditing alleged terrorists to stand trial in Northern Ireland or by allowing the Republic of Ireland to try them in its courts of law never gained acceptance in the respective countries. But the negotiations signaled a willingness on the part of both parties to discuss the fine points of domestic and international law and customs about terrorism and crimes committed abroad.

A decade later, however, the Republic of Ireland softened its opposition because it had gained formal input in Northern Ireland policy. For this change of heart, it took the London government to compromise on Dublin's influence north of its border. The Irish politicians thus could "sell" a revised policy on the emotional subject of extradition of terrorist suspects to British custody. Additionally, the savagery of terrorism in Northern Ireland upended the southern Irish courts' affinity to claims of political status barring extradition of perpetrators involved in particularly heinous bombings.[81]

The pact that brought about these improved relations between London and Dublin was the Anglo-Irish Agreement signed in 1985. This agreement provided consultative rights for the Irish government over British policy on Northern Ireland. While it did not fundamentally alter British policies within the Six Counties, it did secure better cross-border security arrangements for Britain—a critical factor given the mostly porous border. The Protestant loyalist faction interpreted the agreement as a blow to its interests, although it has not turned out that way. Still, loyalist violence picked up in the immediate years following the agreement. The agreement laid the groundwork for Anglo-Irish cooperation because it set up a channel for resolving disputes between the two capitals—that is, set in place a mechanism for calling meetings to discuss issues. This was a breakthrough of sorts, for it helped dispel the lingering animosities of bygone decades.

The agreement also paved the way for the European Parliament, which backed it, to launch an investigation into anti-Catholic discrimination in the province in 1992. The European Parliament gained input into Northern Ireland affairs during the 1990s with the infusion of substantial peace funds. Funding underwrote reconciliation programs, economic development, and cross-border cooperation. One funding program for peace and integration supplied 1.33 billion euros from 1995 to 2006 north and south of the border. Even more European Union monies went to peace programs within Northern Ireland.[82]

Northern Ireland Politics and a Peace Agreement

The political climate within Northern Ireland proved to be difficult to change. British and European funds improved the lives of Catholics and Protestants with jobs, education, housing opportunities, and political representation at district level. Diplomacy brought together ancient rivals by framing a cooperative agreement between the United Kingdom and the Republic of Ireland to defuse conflict in Northern Ireland. But the feelings of resentment and fear resisted amelioration. For too long, parties in Northern Ireland drew backers and built themselves up from the aggrieved in each community. What did change—along with the formation of new political parties—were the attitudes of the two sectarian communities toward their predicament and any resumption of violence in the province. Both Catholics and Protestants experienced a rising standard of living along with prospects for even more improvement in their lives.

These Ulster citizens also took note of the rapid and enormous economic growth in the Republic of Ireland to their immediate south. The Celtic Tiger, as Ireland became known, resembled the heady industrialization and economic liftoff that characterized the so-called Asian Tigers dating from the 1960s. A number of factors contributed to Ireland's stellar development, including favorable tax policies for foreign investment, an educated and receptive labor force, government spending on infrastructure projects to further private sector growth, and, of course, European Union (formerly the European Economic Community) funds and export opportunities.[83] Not wanting to be left behind, people on both sides of the sectarian divide in Northern Ireland longed for a share in the material betterment that their southern brethren enjoyed. That hope—and with the prospect of fulfillment—constituted one of the intangible drivers for a change in attitude in Northern Ireland that laid the groundwork for an end to hostilities.

Working with Dublin, the British Labour Prime Minister Tony Blair issued a declaration allowing in 1993 any political party participation in elections and governing, if it renounced the use of violence. This declaration paved the way for a cessation of violence.

The shaky truce since 1994 played a role in convincing populations on both sides of the sectarian divide that peace was better than three decades of killings and bombings in their midst.

A Republican woman celebrates the IRA ceasefire in Belfast, August 1994. Photo by permission of Newscom.

American involvement in the negotiations between Britain, Ireland, and Northern Ireland parties became an additional factor in leveraging pressure on each to resolve their differences.

Once Bill Clinton settled into the White House, his administration turned to nurturing peace in strife-torn Northern Ireland in fulfillment of one of his campaign promises. Washington interfered in British-Northern Ireland negotiations, raising the ire of Prime Minister Blair, by entertaining visits to the White House by Sinn Fein's Gerry Adams. Clinton also pressured Adams to step away from violence.[84] Laborious negotiations, prodded along by President Clinton's representative former Senator George Mitchell, finally bridged the multifaceted differences in the Good Friday Agreement (also known as the Belfast Agreement), which was signed by Britain and the Republic of Ireland and endorsed by most of the political parties in the Six Counties on 10 April (Good Friday) 1998. It granted Northern Ireland self-rule within the United Kingdom and established a National Assembly. It assured greater civil liberties to the Catholic community along with a reformed judiciary and police service to safeguard the rights.

The complex, 60-page agreement then went before the voters in the Republic of Ireland and Northern Ireland; the results of the referenda overwhelmed expectations, with 71 percent in the North and 94 percent in the South voting yes to it.[85] Elections within Northern Ireland ultimately took place for the assembly; a government formed; and British direct rule of the province came to an end. In the decade since the 1998 agreement's signing, occasional threats, provocations, and even bloodshed disturbed the tranquility in Northern Ireland but the overall stability and peace held.

Peace, if not reconciliation, came to Northern Ireland with the 1998 Good Friday agreement, which grew out of a truce with the mainstream PIRA and enjoyed papal and American support. Hardcore republicanism since the late 1960s had been an urban working-class movement. This PIRA base eroded with the introduction of equality laws and welfarism, which lessened the "ghetto mentality" of working-class Catholics. Electoral politics offered a peaceful, yet unstinting, outlet for Catholic grievances and republican protest that seemed much more attractive than paramilitary violence. Thus, the Sinn Fein opted for elections, seats in parliament, and electoral gains rather than an island-wide republican agenda.[86] Still, the PIRA resisted decommissioning (i.e., disarmament) of its weapons until October 2001, when American and world opinion hardened against terrorism after the

9/11 attacks against the Twin Trade Towers and the Pentagon. Not wanting to be perceived as a terrorist outfit in the new political climate figured powerfully in the PIRA's thinking. Still, this decommissioning process took another four years to complete.

Conclusions

It is the thesis of this narrative that British civic action programs, political arrangements, and the diplomatic initiatives with the Republic of Ireland brought about a cessation of conflict in Northern Ireland. As one astute observer reported:

> By the early 1990s most of the issues on which the Civil Rights Movement had campaigned had been addressed, in part or whole, and the only remaining grievance was that of the nationalists for a united Ireland, a position which even Dublin appeared to be distancing itself from. It may therefore be argued that by the 1990s the British government was, at some level, winning the hearts and minds campaign.[87]

The nonmilitary approaches made a much greater long-range contribution than military counterinsurgency practices of the British Army and its elite units. Readers of the strictly military and counterinsurgency accounts may well place too much emphasis on tactics pursued by the British Army without considering the broader political, economic, social, and diplomatic factors that combined to defuse the violence.

Paul Arthur, a student of the Northern Ireland conflict, wrote that the fighting that began over issues of sovereignty and territory was displaced by politics "more concerned with equity issues."[88] And Jonathan Tonge, another academic observer, noted that "Under an equality agenda, parity of esteem and respect for different identities have displaced the old argument over partition. . . After 3,600 deaths in that conflict, republicans [i.e., Catholics] shelved territorial demands for equality in a state that the IRA sought to dismantle."[89] By addressing the roots of Catholic discontent and discrimination, British governments siphoned off enough anger, enticed enough collaborators, and neutralized enough opposition that it undermined much of the minority's support for IRA violence and led to a peaceful political resolution. The Sinn Fein leadership realized it could not win if its blood-loyal rank-and-file began drifting away to new homes, educational opportunities, and steady jobs.

A cessation of sniping, bombing, and assassinations in Northern Ireland is an enormous achievement after more than 30 years of bloodshed. No one should minimize the attainment of stopping the conflict. But also no one should exaggerate the return to total normalcy. The end of murder and mayhem in Ulster's streets has brought forth a cold peace. Genuine reconciliation between Catholics and Protestants in the province is still a work in progress. To underscore this point, it is noteworthy to acknowledge that the so-called peace walls separating and demarcating the two sectarian zones are now twice as long as they were when the Good Friday agreement was signed in 1998. Lengthening concrete barriers is hardly a positive sign of new-found amity. It demonstrates a fragile, truce-like quality rather than blossoming brotherhood among the two communities. Too much distrust and enmity remain for quick healing. It is also a reminder to outsiders about the intractableness of sectarian battles and the obstacles to attaining genuine reconciliation, after the end of a hot and protracted conflict. Additionally, a few PIRA members and some Protestant loyalists, once peace had been restored, fell back on criminality, such as protection rackets, bank robbery, thuggery, racketeering, and the counterfeiting of currency, watches, and DVDs. And three PIRA members were apprehended for their training of Marxist guerrillas in Colombia. However, the Sinn Fein party broke with violence and pursued a political path to participation in elections and governance with genuine earnest.

A second and perhaps more fundamental point is the uniqueness of Northern Ireland, its history, its culture, and finally its resolution of the internecine fighting. Lessons, techniques, tactics, and strategies that led to the present-day nonbelligerency cannot be applied wholesale to other insurgencies except in the broadest fashion. It would be the height of folly to apply a Northern Ireland template to insurgencies a world away. The common language and culture of counterinsurgency forces and paramilitary forces, the protagonists common roots in Western civilization and modernization, the small population of only 1.5 million residents, and the mostly cooperative assistance from the one neighboring country—the Republic of Ireland—all point to a limited case study in successful counterinsurgency.

Still, the overall picture of the prominence given by British governments in the Northern Ireland case to political settlements, economic incentives (homes, jobs, and education), and amicable relations leading to diplomatic breakthroughs with the adjacent Republic of Ireland—all offer intriguing outlines for the resolution of other insurgencies. Most telling, they point up that economic, political, social, and diplomatic factors—managed by civilian authorities—were in the final analysis the keys to stability and peace. ⬆

Endnotes

Many thanks to Diane Raub for her editing assistance.

1. *The U.S. Army/Marine Corps Counterinsurgency Field Manual* (Chicago: University of Chicago, 2007), page 54.

2. Lieutenant Colonel Robert M. Cassidy, U.S. Army, "The British Army and Counterinsurgency: The Salience of Military Culture," *Military Review* (May-June 2005), page 56.

3. Thomas R. Mockaitis, *British Counterinsurgency, 1919-1960* (New York: St. Martins Press, 1990), page 146.

4. Major General Paul Newton, joint head of Force Strategic Engagement Cell in Iraq, quotation from Colin Freeman, "British General 'to talk to Iraqi insurgents," *Telegraph.co.uk, 12 November 2007.* Downloaded from www.telegraph.co.uk/news/main.jhtm?xml=/news/207/11/11wiraq111.xml; accessed 13 November 2007.

5. A few classic books, such as Robert Thompson, *Defeating Communist Insurgency: The Lessons of Malaya and Vietnam* (New York: Praeger, 1966); David Galula, *Counterinsurgency Warfare: Theory and Practice* (New York: Praeger, 1964); and Thomas H. Henriksen, *Revolution and Counterrevolution: Mozambique's War of Independence, 1964-1974* (Westport, Connecticut: Greenwood Press, 1983) and for the less studied rural conflict in then-Rhodesia, Lewis H. Gann and Thomas H. Henriksen, *The Struggle for Zimbabwe: Battle in the Bush* (New York: Praeger Publishers, 1981).

6. Kalev I. Sepp, "Best Practices in Counterinsurgency," *Military Review* (May-June 2005), pages 8-12.

7. Thomas H. Henriksen, *The Israeli Approach to Irregular Warfare and Implication for the United States*, JSOU Report 07-3 (2007).

8. Thomas R. Mockaitis, "The Iraq War: Learning from the Past, Adapting to the Present, and Planning for the Future," series from the Amery War College Strategic Studies Institute (February 2007), page 19. Downloaded from www.strategicstudiesinstitute.army.mil/pdffiles/PUB754.pdf; accessed 25 August 2008.

9. Robert M. Cassidy, *Counterinsurgency and the Global War on Terror: Military Culture and Irregular War* (Westport, Connecticut: Praeger, 2006), page 92.

10. Gavin Bulloch, "Military Doctrine and Counter-Insurgency: A British Perspective," *Parameters* 26 (Summer 1996), page 4.

11. Robert M. Cassidy, "The British Army and Counterinsurgency: The Salience of Culture," *Military Review* (May-June, 2005), page 55.

12. Cecil Woodham-Smith, *The Reason Why: The Story of the Fatal Charge of the Light Brigade* (New York: McGraw-Hill, 1953), page 116.

13. Evelyn Waugh, *Sword of Honour* (London: Penguin Books, 1965), page 34.

14. For one easily accessible biography of Wingate, see Leonard Mosley, *Gideon Goes to War* (London: Arthur Barker, 1955).

15. Michael Calvert, *Chindits: Long Range Penetration* (New York: Ballentine Books, 1973), pages 10-11.

16. J. Paul de B. Taillon, *The Evolution of Special Forces in Counter-Terrorism: The British and American Experiences* (Westport, Connecticut: Praeger, 2001), page 7.

17. No author but a foreword by Louis Mountbatten, *Combined Operations: The Official Story of the Commandos* (New York: Macmillan Co., 1943).

18. John A. Nagl, *Learning to Eat Soup with a Knife: Counterinsurgency Lessons from Malaya and Vietnam* (Westport, Connecticut: Praeger, 2002), pages 192-197.

19. Robert Thompson, *Defeating Communist Insurgency: The Lessons of Malaya and Vietnam* (New York: Frederick A. Praeger, 1966).

20. Brian Lapping, *End of Empire* (London: Paladin Grafton, 1985), page 224.

21. Cornelius Tacitus, *Agricola and Germany*, translated by Anthony R. Birley (Oxford, United Kingdom: Oxford University Press, 1999), page 22.

22. *Caesar: The Conquest of Gaul*, translated by S. A. Handford (London: Penguin Books, 1951), pages 60 and 64.

23. Mockaitis, "Low-Intensity Conflict: The British Experience," *Conflict Quarterly*, page 8.

24. Robert Cassidy, "British Army and Counterinsurgency," page 56.

25. *Ibid.*, 59.

26. Cassidy, *Counterinsurgency and the Global War on Terror*, page 89.

27. John Keegan, *The Iraq War* (London: Hutchinson, 2004), pages 175-176.

28. Warren Chin, "Examining the Application of British Counterinsurgency Doctrine by the American Army in Iraq," *Small Wars and Insurgency*, Vol. 18, No. 1 (March, 2007), page 22.

29. Stephen Farrell, "Divining A Lesson In Basra," *New York Times*, 25 May 2008, section IV, page A1.; John Burns, "Britain Debates Army's Delay at Basra, *New York Times*, 7 August 2008, page A12; Michael Evans, "Sidelined British Soldiers 'itched to join' U.S. fight for Basra," *London Times*, 7 August 2008, page 1; Jonathan Finer, "An End to the Soft Sell by the British in Basra," *Washington Post*, 26 February 2006, page A16; Karen DeYoung and Thomas E. Ricks, "As British Leave, Basra Deteriorates," *Washington Post*, 7 August 2008, page A1; and Deborah Haynes and Richard Beeston, "Time To Go Home, Iraqi Leader Tells Britain," *London Times*, 3 October 2008, page 3.

30. Carlotta Gall, "Optimism Grows as Marines Push against Taliban," *New York Times*, 27 May 2008, page A1.

31. Aidan Clarke, "The Colonisation of Ulster and The Rebellion of 1641," in *The Course of Irish History*, eds. T. W. Moody and F. X. Martin (Cork, Ireland: Mercier Press, 1984), pages 190-193.

32. E. R. R. Green, "The Great Famine," in *The Course of Irish History*, ed. T. W. Moody and F. X. Martin (Cork, Ireland: Mercer Press, 1984), pages 273-274.

33. Tony Geraghty, *The Irish War: The Hidden Conflict between the IRA and British Intelligence* (Baltimore: Johns Hopkins University Press, 1998), pages 172, 177, and 210 and Kevin Kelley, *The Longest War: Northern Ireland and the IRA* (Westport, Connecticut: Lawrence Hill & Co., 1982), pages 135-136 and 277.

34. Cecil Woodham-Smith, *The Great Hunger: Ireland 1845-1849* (New York: Signet Books, 1962).

35. Walter L. Arnstein, *Britain Yesterday and Today* (Lexington, Massachusetts: D.C. Heath and Company, 1971), pages 237-380.

36. Charles Townsend, *British Campaign in Ireland, 1919-1921: The Development of Political and Military Strategy* (New York: Oxford University Press, 1975), page 206.

37. Lawrence J. McCaffrey, *Ireland from Colony to Nation State* (Englewood Cliffs, New Jersey: Prentice-Hall, 1979), pages 148-150.

38. Thomas Hennessey, *A History of Northern Ireland*, 1920-1996 (Dublin: Gill & Macmillan, 1997), page 115.

39. McCaffrey, *Ireland from Colony to Nation State*, page 175.

40. Paul Bew, Peter Gibbon, and Henry Patterson, *Northern Ireland, 1921-1994: Political Forces and Social Classes* (London: Serif, 1995), pages 115-118.

41. *Disturbances in Northern Ireland: Report of the Committee Appointed by the Governor of Northern Ireland* (Belfast: Her Majesty's Stationery Office, 1960), pages 88-89. Download from http://cain.ulst.ac.uk/hmso/cameron.htm; accessed on 19 August 2008.

42. Hennessey, *A History of Ireland*, pages 129-130.

43. Paul Arthur, *Special Relationships: Britain, Ireland and the Northern Ireland Problem* (Belfast: Blackstaff Press, 2000), page 36.

44. Michael J. Cunningham, *British Government Policy in Northern Ireland, 1969-1989: Its Nature and Execution* (Manchester: Manchester University Press, 1991), page 25.

45. Brendan O'Leary and John McGarry, *The Politics of Antagonism: Understanding Northern Ireland* (London: Athlone Press, 1993), page 197.

46. J. Bowyer Bell, "An Irish War," *Small Wars and Insurgencies*, Vol. 1, No. 3 (December 1990), page 124.

47. Thomas Harding, "British Brigadier Attacks American's John Wayne Generals," *London Daily Telegraph*, 19 April 2006, page 1.

48. Geraghty, *The Irish War*, pages 74-76 and 116-119.

49. Raymond Murray, *The SAS in Ireland* (Dublin: Mercier Press, 1990), pages 426-430 and 441-443.

50. One recent article from a British officer offered a more balanced assessment of the political and economic aspects of securing reconciliation. See, John Clark, "Northern Ireland: A Balanced Approach to Amnesty, Reconciliation, and Reintegration," *Military Review* (January-February 2008), pages 37-49.

51. John Keegan, *Iraq War*, page 175.

52. Michael Dewar, *The British Army in Northern Ireland* (London: Arms and Armour Press, 1985), page 228.

53. Jonathan Tonge, *Northern Ireland* (Cambridge, United Kingdom: Polity Press, 2006), page 71.

54. Dewar, *British Army in Northern Ireland*, page 223.

55. Martin Van Creveld, *The Changing Face of War: Lessons of Combat, from the Marne to Iraq* (New York: Ballantine Books, 2006), pages 233-234.

56. Tonge, *Northern Ireland*, pages 85-88.

57. Tim Ripley, *Security Forces in Northern Ireland, 1969-1992* (London: Osprey Publishing, 1993), page 8.

58. *Digest of Statistics Northern Ireland, No. 51* (Belfast: Her Majesty's Stationery Office, March 1979), page 87.

59. Mike Tomlinson, "Relegating Local Government," in Liam O'Dowd, Bill Rolston, and Mike Tomlinson, *Northern Ireland: Between Civil Rights and Civil War* (London: CSE Books, 1980), pages 116-117.

60. Ed Moloney, *A Secret History of the IRA* (London: Penguin Press, 2002), pages 241-243.

61. Sean Kennedy and Derek Birrell, "Housing" in John Darby and Arthur Williamson, eds. *Violence and the Social Services in Northern Ireland* (London: Heinemann, 1978), page 99.

62. David Singleton, "Northern Ireland Housing: Number One Priority but for How Much Longer?" in *Housing Review*, Vol. 35, No. 2 (1986), pages 48-49.

63. Michael McKernan, editor, *Northern Ireland Yearbook 2003: A Comprehensive Reference Guide to the Political, Economic, and Social Life of Northern Ireland* (Belfast: BMF Publishing, 2002), page 282.

64. John Henry Whyte, *Interpreting Northern Ireland* (Oxford: Clarendon Press, 1990), pages 55-56.

65. Kevin Boyle and Tom Hadden, *Northern Ireland: The Choice* (New York: *Penguin Books*, 1994), pages 45-46.

66. Michael J. Cunningham, *British Government Policy in Northern Ireland, 1969-1989; Its Nature and Execution* (Manchester: Manchester University Press, 1991), page 159.

67. Paul Bew and Gordon Gillespie, *The Northern Ireland Peace Process, 1993-1996: A Chronology* (London: Serif, 1996), page 141.

68. Hennessey, *A History of Northern Ireland*, page 240.

69. McKernan, *Northern Ireland Yearbook 2003*, page 331.

70. Hennessey, *A History of Northern Ireland*, pages 240-241.

71. McKernan. *Northern Ireland Yearbook 2003*, page 382.

72. James Lyons, "Economic Development and Peacebuilding in Northern Ireland," public lecture, Stanford Law School, 28 February 2008.

73. Derick Wilson and Jerry Tyrrell, "Institutions for Conciliation and Mediation," in Seamus Dunn, editor, *Facets of the Northern Ireland Conflict* (New York: St. Martins Press, 1995), pages 230-233 and 241-243.

74. Alan Smith, "Education and the Conflict in Northern Ireland," *Facets of the Conflict in Northern Ireland*, edited by Seamus Dunn (London: Macmillan, 1995), pages 172-173.

75. *Ibid*, 178-179.

76. Table 2.2 "Current expenditures on social services and housing by the central government," *Northern Ireland Annual Abstract of Statistics* (Belfast: Her Majesty's Stationery Office, 1982), page 15.

77. *Digest of Statistics, Northern Ireland, No. 51* (Belfast: Her Majesty's Stationery Office, March 1979), page 25.

78. FN: Table 4.7 "Further Education: Vocational Courses; students and teaching staff," *Northern Ireland Annual Abstract of Statistics* (Belfast: Her Majesty's Stationery Office, 1982), page 44.

79. Table 2.2 "Current expenditures on social services and housing by the central government," *Northern Ireland Annual Abstract of Statistics* (Belfast: Her Majesty's Stationery Office, 1982), page 15.

80. Peter Taylor, *Loyalists: War and Peace in Northern Ireland* (New York: TV Books, 1999), page 234.

81. Cunningham, *British Government Policy in Northern Ireland 1969-89*, page 207.

82. Jonathan Tonge, *Northern Ireland* (Cambridge, United Kingdom: Polity Press, 2006), page 36.

83. Ray MacSharry and Padraic A. White, *The Making of the Celtic Tiger: The Inside Story of Ireland's Boom Economy* (Dublin: Mercier Press, 2000), pages 147-161.

84. Bill Clinton, *My Life* (New York: Alfred A. Knopf, 2004), pages 578-581.

85. The Good Friday Agreement, Northern Ireland Office site, www.nio.gov.uk/the-agreement. Downloaded 2 September 2008.

86. Tonge, *Northern Ireland*, page 128.

87. Collin McInnes, *Hot War, Cold War: The British Army's Way in Warfare, 1945-1995* (London: Brassey's, 1996), page 169.

88. Paul Arthur, *Special Relationships: Britain, Ireland, and the Northern Ireland Problem* (Belfast: Blackstaff Press, 2000), page 249.

89. Tonge, *Northern Ireland*, page 37.